Sales Success for the Seasoned -Sales Veteran

How to Gain a Strategic Edge and Close More Sales, More Often!

by Stephen P. Lentini

Copyright© 2009 by Stephen P. Lentini

All rights reserved. No part of this book may be reproduced without the permission in writing from the author, except by a reviewer who may quote brief passages or reproduce illustrations in a review with appropriate credit; nor may any part of this book be reproduced, stored in a retrieval system, or transmitted in any form or by any means – electronic, photocopying, recording, or other – without permission in writing from the publisher.

Permission, write the publisher:
Stephen Lentini
Sales Leadership
146 N Main St, Unit 1
St. Albans, VT 05478

Produced in the United States of America by *Pop Color*, Williston, Vermont

Table of Contents

Acknowledgments 4

Forward 5

Chapters:

Section 1

    1. Stay Certain of Success 9
    2. Identify needs 13
    3. Let them say no first 18
    4. Give more but don't over promise 23
    5. Get to Know them better 25
    6. Let it be 29
    7. Get an appropriate price 31
    8. Develop a system 37
    9. Sales are flat and Feeling stuck, what to do?

Section 2 "Seeds of Success"

    10. Seeds of Success 41
    11. Set Time and Boundaries 46
    12. Deal Cheerfully with Objections and Complaints 50
    13. When Prospecting and Networking, Use Your Contacts Develop New Behaviours/Love Being Better Than You Were Yesterday 56
    14. Develop new behaviours/Love being better than you were yesterday 62
    15. Remember that "What goes around comes around" 66
    16. Motivate, Motivate, Motivate 71

17. Dream and believe in Possibilities 73
18. Integrity, keep your word, do what you said.................. 76
19. Stop the Whining attitude and
    Start the Winning attitude 79
20. Be Grateful everyday... 82
21. We do live in a Galaxy, in a universe............................. 83
22. Gaining and Keeping an Edge to Close More Sales, More Often
23. Business Strategy Coaching for the company and for the team.
24. **Managing the Culture for Growth*** excerpt from "Lightning Growth" by Justin Sachs and this chapter is by Steve Lentini pages 224-231

Conclusion... 89

Acknowledgments

"Thanks to all my friends and family for the encouragement along the way"

~ Steve

Forward

A few thoughts to prepare the ground

Seeds of the Sale

Selling with Integrity

This book is about staying at peak performance in sales and succeeding. Selling is about being in relationship. People buy from people they like and trust. It's about breaking through barriers to succeeding after you have been in sales for many years. This may not be you… and I have worked with hundreds of sales people who are very talented and yet for some reason go stale in their sales career. This book will help you see the blocks in yourself that are keeping you from reaching your goals year after year with the same excitement that you had at the start. This book is about the role that integrity plays in selling.

If you sell with Integrity and you sell your truth, people will like and trust you. You will attract what you require in life. Who wouldn't recommend or buy from someone whose reputation is one of integrity? Whose main interest is in serving their higher calling by working to serve those that they sell? Or from someone who would walk away from a sale because they see that the solution or conditions are not a fit for either of them in the long term?

Selling from integrity means listening for what would best serve the customer and not our next bonus or commission. It means living true to our higher calling, listening to our soul and doing what is "in integrity", the best for all concerned.

In this book, you will learn how to gain the respect and admiration of your customers and prospects by letting your true and real self out. You can be yourself in selling if you learn what behaviour to control and which behaviour to emphasize on a sales call and in any relationship in life. You can let go of worry over quota's, you can stop trying to manipulate others or trying to think of the "next clever thing to say." No need to sell anything if you are listening for what would solve your customers or prospects problems. If you are listening to see if they are a fit for your company and you are willing to let them go, to another solution or to a competitor if you are not the best fit, prospects will buy.

You will learn how to relax and let your customer sell himself. You will learn how to walk him to that sale. You will learn to stop doing business with people who don't respect you. You will learn how to command respect and sell more.

Selling should be fun and what's more fun than being in control of your life, your destiny and you're self. After all, the only thing you can control is you and that's what this book will focus on. As you change, things change. I often say that "If you don't like your experience of the world, change how the world is experiencing you."

Learning how to communicate to improve your sales is one path to take. Improved communication by itself is not enough. Learning what has been holding you back is the key. I managed salespeople for many years, over 20 in fact, and I have conducted sales training courses for over 19 years. The one thing that I observed over and over was that, even salespeople that had great communication skills, "hit the wall" and fell short of their goals. The reason; they focused on things outside of themselves to fix the problem… **when they were the problem. The great motivational speaker and author Jim Rohn once said, "The harder I worked on myself, the better my business did."**

In this book, you will learn how to begin the journey of working on your "self." How to take your "self" on. That is what I teach in all of my classes. Training on better ways to sell is a positive thing. Training yourself to see your "default patterns" will add more happiness, joy, fulfilment and money than sales training alone, in the long run.

Adding a "Higher Power" to your life is a necessary component as well. Remember, we do live in a galaxy, in a Universe. You can honour your higher calling through your work. You can bring your soul with you to work. In this book, you will learn how to add a "spiritual power", an enlightened way of thinking, one that will add an ease and satisfaction to your work. If practiced, you will find joy and satisfaction, while you reach your goals. You will also learn to understand and plan using the "seasons", just like nature has seasons, there are seasons in sales. You will learn about the Universal Laws of Success. Studied by many successful people, I build upon the work by Napoleon Hill, Wayne Dyer, Deepak Chopra, Jim Rohn and many others who have written about the Laws of Success.

"Selling can be fun and easy when you go with the flow."

"Going with the flow" is a new concept to grasp. The words, "going with the flow" invoke an uncomfortable feeling in most type "A" sales people. They believe that everything happens in response to some action that they take. They have the attitude of "always be closing." They feel it is necessary to keep the "pressure on" by having the next greatest thing to say that will close the prospect. Prospects who have

been helped to buy properly won't have to be closed. Don't get me wrong, action in sales is a necessary thing and many good results come from action. **Albert Einstein once said "nothing happens until something moves."** "Going with the flow" doesn't imply, not to take action. What I mean by saying "go with the flow", it's developing an intuitive sense of what to do next. Going with the flow is paying attention to how you "feel" during a sales call or in any situation and finding a way to say what you are "feeling" Dave Sandler of Sandler Sales Institute always said, "If you feel it, find a way to say it" I say, "Always sell the truth, and if the truth won't sell, don't sell it."

Tip: If you have to lie to make a sale……. don't.

You sense by how the conversation is going, what a prospects body language, tone and expressions are telling you, what the necessary next steps are. You are helping the prospect or customer by allowing them space to have their feelings and opinions and in return the prospect builds a stronger sense of trust and comfort with you. Sales increase, customer bonds are stronger and longer lasting if you can learn to "go with the flow."

I learned selling with integrity by always being honest, and noticing how prospects responded so enthusiastically to me, if they did not buy that day, often they did buy or call me later. Many time prospects called after the company they did business with showed them a lack of integrity. I also learned by having a lack of integrity in my personal life, that it cost me. I was able to "wake up" and notice the difference in my integrity with clients and customers and how it served me well and what the cost was, of my lack of integrity in my personal life. Now, applying the laws of integrity in all of my life has had amazing benefits. When I changed, thing changed. The common denominator, in all of my life situations, was me.

I've witnessed and worked with sales people, over the years that made their job so much more difficult. The main reason for their difficulty was that they never shut up long enough to listen to their customers. Their customers were telling them the secret to selling them. Some of these "so-called salespeople" - loved hearing themselves so much they never stopped talking long enough to observe great salespeople at work, and they never absorbed another way of doing things. In fact - they thought they were so great, they never asked successful people what it was that they could do to be more successful. So - here it is - if you want it - all the information you'll ever need to keep selling with integrity.

1. Stay Certain of Success

Think positive thoughts about yourself and the prospect. Do you remember a time when you sensed a friend, spouse, co-worker or your child seemed down or blue? Can you tell when someone has a great attitude? Is really enthused about something? We can all sense how others around us are feeling and this goes for your prospects. They can sense the same about you. The entire universe is energy. Your thoughts are energy. Project only the best energy by disciplining your thoughts before you go into a sales call. I salute the "Divinity" within all of the people that I meet each day. I am always thinking and disciplining my thoughts. In fact, practice disciplining your thoughts at all times and it will be second nature in a sales call. The side benefit will be that the world around you will change as you change your thinking. **Earl Nightingale said "you become what you think about."**

Notice now, what is it that dominates your thoughts all day long? Napoleon Hill, in "Think and grow Rich", suggests writing out what you desire with a designated time frame that you will accomplish it by, add what you will give**, (giving is key to receiving in life) and what you intend to do with your desire and to read it every morning and evening, when you get up and before you go to bed.** I personally use this method, along with visualization, meditation and affirmations every day. All of these ingredients have added immense success to my life along with joy and satisfaction.

*TIP: You are what you think about.
Notice your predominant thought patterns.

Regardless of how you are feeling, **act as if** you are confident. Change your body language to reflect how a confident person would carry themselves; walk like a confident person would walk. By **acting as if** you are confident, you will notice that in a short time you will feel confident. Those around you will sense that confidence.

If you have a belief in a "Higher Power", the Divine or God, you can bring a miracle power, into your sales call, your work day that "nothing (no thing) is out of order in the Universe..." And that is so in your life. Spend some time each day in silence and listen to what your soul is telling you. The "Master is Within, Life is the Teacher." Pay attention to your inner self. Follow those intuitions, feelings that come from nowhere. Wayne Dyer says, "everything in the Universe came from no- where, now here." Follow those prompts. Pay attention to the results of following those prompts. I use a journal to record what happens when I follow my intuition...those thoughts that come from no-where. Prove to yourself that intuition is guidance from your Higher Self, the Universal energy, your soul, whatever you choose to call it...prove it.

Even if you do not believe in a Higher Power, no-thing is out of order anyway...how could it be....? How would earth remain suspended in the midst of darkness, with all that is required for life right here now, if anything was out of order? There is something that is keeping the planets orbiting in perfect order, keeping the Universe from flying apart. As Deepak Chopra says in his book "Power, Freedom and Grace" "When you have a conscious awareness of your soul, you experience everything as a miracle."

Remember when you feel that things are out of control to surrender to the idea that things are happening as they should. As Eckert Tolle says in his book "The Power of Now", "there is only now." When you accept the moment, you create space for something new, perhaps a miracle to appear. Eckert also says "when you fight life, life fights you."

Pay attention to what you can do that is in your control. You cannot control others, so release them. You focus on you. The serenity prayer says "God, grant me the serenity to accept the things I cannot change, the courage to change the things I can and the wisdom to know the difference." If you are willing to surrender to what is and focus only on what you can change, you are left with the energy to work with all your gifts and talents. You will be happy because, knowing that you have done your best, you let the rest go. You will be amazed at the dimension of joy that is added to your life as a result. People around you will notice your peaceful demeanor as well. Clients and prospects will notice too and bringing this kind of thinking to your work will affect your results positively.

Thoughts are things. Lynne McTaggert in her book "The Intention Experiment" says "Dozens of scientists have produced thousands of papers in the scientific literature offering sound evidence that thought is capable of profoundly affecting all aspects of our lives." As observers and creators, we are constantly remaking our world at every instant. Every thought we have, every judgment we hold, however unconscious, is having an effect. With every moment that it notices, the conscious mind is sending an intention. Pay attention to your thoughts. Forward your aim to your desired result, intend its outcome. Visualize the outcome and feel what it will feel like to get it…see the rewards…see the happy clients faces…see the $$$$$ that will come your way.

Notice too, what has been your predominant thought pattern and does it match what you are currently harvesting in your life? I do not even know you and I would say without a doubt the answer is yes. Otherwise, who is creating this result? Are you a circumstance in your life or the creator of your experience? The choice is yours and your world will form around that choice.

I prefer to be the creator and not the circumstance. Think about it and make the conscious choice from today forward to intend what you want to create and to create from what you intend. Do not let anything or anyone deter you. When thoughts of doubt appear…send them packing. When others who doubt, your choices appear (and they will, they are after all reflections of your own doubt), send them packing as well.

My teacher, Toni Stone says "Remember too, that things will not appear to be as you want them, until they are." This is the argument for perseverance. Stick with it no matter what.

Even if you do not believe in God or an Infinite Intelligence, if you are an atheist…you can bring "positive energy", positive thoughts with you on your sales calls and with you at all times. The Universe is teeming with energy…you are energy and thoughts have energy. How is it that on the phone someone else can detect if we are feeling down? Or perhaps you have noticed that when you have called someone that they are agitated or depressed? How is it that you noticed? You heard it in their voice. Your energy level can be detected in person and on the phone. Bring positive thoughts and the great energy associated with positive thinking with you in every moment and watch your success skyrocket.

If your sales are flat for an extended period or you are not feeling motivated, look at your behaviour as well. Have you made new call this week? This month? This year? You are creating your world, so there is no need to express here who is the creator of this? If you are not feeling motivated it's time to think back to the time when you were. What is the difference? Were you more grateful for simple things? Were you excited because it was a new challenge? Perhaps it's time to create your own challenges daily…or for each month, quarter and year. Set the bar higher for yourself? Ask you existing customers what they like about you? Start out each day with the people who like you. If you cannot energize yourself by changing your thinking, then change your routine. Who are you surrounding yourself with? Are you hanging around successful people who push you? Challenge you? If not, perhaps that is one change to make as soon as possible. Love them from afar and make new friends. You are now, the sum total of all your thoughts, word and actions. The people you surround yourself with are a reflection of you. If they are not motivated and ambitious, then guess what? Neither are you.

If you don't like your experience of the world, change how the world is experiencing you" Steve Lentini

Brian Tracy has said that he progressed after every lesson he learned about himself. Study successful people, take seminars, read and or listen to work that inspires you. You will slowly pull yourself out of the funk you are in by continually working on yourself.

Begin experimenting with what energy and thoughts you focus on daily. See what result positive thinking and disciplined thinking brings you. Discover your own power to create after all, you have created this stuck period.

2. Ask them what their needs are and make a purchase happen

You do not want everyone for a customer; you only want "good" customers. (Good customers make a good company - and a good commission.) The only way to determine which of the many prospects you want for customers is to let them to tell you about their company and needs, they can't do this if you are doing the talking. (You'll have plenty of time to tell them all about your company later.) Prepare questions before the call that will help you get useful information and allow you to match good prospects with your company's strengths. Remember Who, What, Where, When, Why and How? Some examples are; "What do you look for in a supplier?" "What issues or challenges are you facing in your business that you see us helping you with?" "Of those things that you just shared which in most important?" "Which is least important?"

If they tell you about any issues with one of their suppliers, some other great questions to ask are;

"How long have you been dealing with this….?" (If they answer this with Oh, a long, long time, it probably means that they are not motivated to fix the problem). "What if we fixed 85% of the issue……?" "What if we could only fix 50% of the……?" "How would you fix the issue?" These questions help you understand if the prospect has realistic expectations about solving the problem.

Use past, present, future, as suggested by author and sales trainer, Steve Schiffman. "Please give me some history on this issue…what were your biggest challenges in the past? Today, any issues? And now? What about going forward? How do see the future if you do not fix this now? In the past, how have you addressed these issues? Presently how are you dealing with ……? For you, with this issue, what is the ideal future solution when it comes to ……? Other good questions are "What are some of your goals for the company / department this year?" "How could we help you achieve those goals?" Use their last experience with change…ask "the last time you made a software change, what happened? What did you learn that you would like to avoid with this upcoming change? What scares you most about this change today? What if you stayed the same? What would happen?

Take notes…. listen and look for gestures, expressions of emotion on these answers…. if there is none…perhaps they are just shopping…you could ask… "I could be wrong and I sense there is no real urgency to deal with this issue just now…?"

TIP: You could say "no" too…. remember, not everyone is a fit.

If you see or feel a lot of emotion with some of the responses, you could say…. "I noticed that you were really expressive when I asked xxxxxx…tell me more about that" …. The emotion indicates that you have struck a nerve, a real issue for him or her…. if you have the best solution here, you are on the way to making the sale. Keep asking questions and listen to what they would do to fix it…and then ask.

"What if I had 80% of that solution?" Again, listen…. then you could ask…." What is your budget to fix the problem?" Making sure here that they are realistic about the investment to fix the problem and that it fits your pricing structure.

Understanding what makes your prospect special in the marketplace or in their eyes could be important to determining if you can help this prospect, so ask questions like "What separates you from your competition?" or "where are you planning to take the company in the marketplace?"

Also, the right questions, tactfully asked, such as "How many deliveries do you require?" and "What's your company's average time frame for invoice payment?" will help you structure viable business deals for good customers and discourage frustrating habits such as late payments, small orders, last minute deliveries, etc. Use the Covey method. **Stephen Covey suggests "in anything that we want to achieve, start with the end in mind."** Whatever industry you are in or service you provide, start with what is the ideal prospect or customer for you. Then create the questions that would provide you with the information to determine if the interview is going your way. You have the right to determine if prospects are really committed to changing.

**TIP: Help people buy, selling is dead.*

Owning this information also allows you to walk away from customers that have no business acumen. Remember to listen carefully to the answers and don't hesitate to take notes. If you can't recall the answers when you need them, why ask?

The most important part of selling, is to keep your focus on the prospect or customer. When others are doing the talking we are most likely to learn how to sell someone or what would they buy.

**TIP: Your job is to GET INFORMATION, not give it!*

If you are asking questions the prospect is speaking and your job is to get information not to give it. The prospect should be talking 60 – 75% of the time. If they are, fine, you are doing your job. If not and you notice that you are doing most of the talking, stop…. And start asking the questions. If you have prepared before the call, thinking about what you would like to know about the prospect and you learn to follow a system on a sales call, then your success ratio will improve. Following a system will help you stay on track. I will help you develop a system later in this book.

Relationship skills are key

Doing business is a relationship and relationships are defined as two or more people. Certainly, you will have people that you will not want to do business with.

The only way to determine which prospects you want for customers is to let them tell you about their company and their needs.

Also, use questions to help you achieve more in life, to reach your goals, ask for help.

Everything that we require in this life comes from someone else. Asking is the key to getting what we want. Many of us feel that if we are not working hard, we are not really doing anything worthwhile or that "things just do not come easy to us." That is how I used to feel. Working hard distracted me from dealing with my real feelings. Working hard is how I used to determine my self-worth. I would never ask anyone for help because it was a sign of weakness. It meant that I had to admit that this (whatever it was) project or problem was something that I could not do or solve myself. I now realize how this kind of thinking held me back. I changed my mind and thinking about asking for help. I could ask for the order and not for help. ***I ask for help all the time now. I ask for referrals, for ideas and suggestions on how they would grow the business if they were me, for help with a new contact, etc.***

My life has changed significantly for the better. People love to help. I was always willing to help others and did help many people, yet I was unwilling to ask for help for myself. I remember refusing help offered by others who obviously could see that I was struggling with something. Besides asking questions of prospects and customers to help you sell easily, remember to ask for help with achieving your goals and daily tasks.

Oh, and by the way, don't forget to ask for the business. Use a thermometer to take the temperature of your prospects. Ask, "on a scale of 1 to 10 if 1 was you were not convinced that we had the solution to your problem and 8 was you would move to the next step, where are you on that scale?" If the answer is five, six or seven, ask "what would you need to hear to get to an 8?" Listen very intently here, because they are going to tell you how to get the order. You can then say "what if I could get you 85% of that…?" (under promise and over deliver, you can always give them 90% or more of what they want and pleasantly surprise them) "what would happen next?" Again, listen intently, you might hear something like "Well, if you could do that, when would you start…?" (buying signal). Listen for buying signals.

On the other hand, if the answer to your "on a scale of 1 to 8" question you hear a "one, two, three or four, do not panic, (after all, you can't lose what you don't have), you could say "well, I must have missed something, is there anything that I could say that would get you to a five…?" Again, listen intently. You could also say, "Well, I must have missed something, do you mind if I review with you what you just told me about the issue…?" And then go over your notes. Confirm what they told you and ask what you are missing. If it is no, fine. Ask what you could have done better before you go. At least get a lesson if you cannot get the order. Ask also, do they mind if you check in with them from time to time...? If you have made them comfortable, perhaps they will buy from you in the future.

Ask and prepare questions, starting with the end in mind from now on and follow it. You will be amazed at the results.

**TIP: "you can help them make a purchase,
the best purchase for them and that is being in integrity"*

When it's your turn to speak, and it will be your turn at some point, address only the needs or concerns that they shared with you. If you have questioned and listened well, you will know by now if your product or service is a fit for your prospect. Help your prospects make the proper buying decision. If the truth won't sell, don't sell it. Product knowledge is wonderful, but save it for after you've gotten enough information about filling a need or solving a problem. **Jeffrey Gittomer says in his book titled "The Little Red Book of Selling", "They don't want your sales pitch. They want answers to their situations and concerns."**

If your product or service will not answer their concerns or address their needs, then tell them. Educate them on what your strengths are and let them decide if they would like to continue at this point. You could say, "We're not the best at addressing x, although we are, as our customers tell us, very good at y" What should we do now? Should we continue?" If they say yes, you could ask, "Gee, if we're not a really good fit for x, then I'm curious, how come you would like to hear about y.

It important here that you are really feeling curious, I know that I would be. If you feel something, find a way to say it. Listen intertly and take notes on their answer, your honesty paves the way for a better relationship and provides a way for the prospect to trust you. If you cannot help them now, believe me, they will be glad to invite you in later when other opportunities arise. Prospects will also stretch their current opportunity to match your strengths where feasible because of the trust you are building by selling honesty.

That's why I say, if the truth won't sell, don't sell it.

**TIP: Be authentic, forget commissions
and sell solutions to problems, even if the solution is not yours.*

3. Be Upfront and Go for No

How many sales people are comfortable going for no? We worry about rejection. We cannot relax. Starting at no is more fun and it takes the pressure off of both of you.

*TIP: You cannot lose what you do not have

Instead of going for no early, we let the customer have control of the sale and we waste time and resources in calls that are going nowhere. We wait and wonder if the customer finds value in what we say.

Let me suggest a different approach. Give your customer/prospect the opportunity to say no and watch what happens. I suggest that 70 - 80% of the time that the real dialogue will begin after the first no.

Here is an example of giving you customer or prospect the opportunity to say no –

"Thank you Mr. / Ms. Prospect for inviting me in. I have prepared an agenda for our time together. Do you mind if I review it? I'm going to ask you some questions about your company and then you can ask me about mine. If after our exchange, you **cannot** see a reason for our two companies to get together **for now, for this moment,** would you mind sharing that with me? I am ok with it. If on the other hand, you do see a reason to move forward, would you let me know that as well? Then together we can determine what the next step will be. Are you okay with that?"

Giving your prospect the opportunity to say no is refreshing. A sales person who is trying to take the pressure off of them will surprise them.

*TIP: No is a sales person's friend, relax at no,
go with it and find GOLD!

If they say no, ask them why? Listen carefully. Your true selling starts here.

For example, if after your questions, you ask "Well Mr. /Ms. Prospect, have you heard or seen any reason for me to continue?" If they respond no, now ask, "May I ask why?" Let's suppose the prospect responds with "Well I'm happy with my current supplier and I'm not going to change." You could respond with "I appreciate that; under what circumstances would you consider a change?" **Listen** - or you might say, "I hear that you are happy with your current supplier however no one is perfect. In fact, we're not, but if you had a magic wand, what, if anything would you improve about your current supplier?"

Do you see what I am saying? Even after you get a no, you have established dialogue after the no, with questions. It's the dialogue you want. Look for openings in their answers to your questions - listen carefully.

If it is really **no, you have shortened the selling cycle,** and now you can move on to more prospects sooner. Remember to remind them that no was for now. Ask if they mind if you return from time to time if you have an idea or suggestion for them. Ask them what kind of ideas or suggestions would they appreciate? What areas of their business are they looking for ideas on?

They will respect your approach and invite you back.

Whatever your concerns are, come up with a question that deals with the issue up front and wait for the answer. You will never need a "tacky tactic" if you are saying what you are feeling. Find a way to say it. If you are feeling uncomfortable about bringing something up, say that you are feeling uncomfortable about something and you wondered if you could bring up something that they might find uncomfortable.

Whatever your fears are, find a way to bring them up as well. If someone asks for your pricing early in the sales call, you might fear that they are just shopping to compare and give your pricing to their current supplier...if you feel that, you would say "my biggest fear is that if I give you a price list now, you will bring it to your current supplier just to lower your pricing, I have had that happen before and maybe that is not the case here...could it be the reason you are asking for pricing just now?"

Remember my acronym for FEAR, **F**acing "**E**normous" **A**dversity **R**ealistically/**R**esponsibly. When we feel fear, it is an indicator from our body that some action is required on our part. Face, it. Walk into it. I put the word "Enormous" in quotes because often when we fear something, we have made it enormous. And when we get to the other side of the issue, we look back and "why did I fear that, it was not a big deal after all. I say realistically/responsibly as some situations call for common sense. If your personal safety is involved for example, "realistically" would mean get out of there. Responsibly would mean to be sure that our response is with integrity, that we do the right thing.

**TIP: Remember FEAR;*
Facing "Enormous" Adversity Realistically/Responsibly

If you notice that something you said may have upset the prospect, bring it up. You could say, I'm feeling like I have said something that upset you, is that the case?

If the prospect says something that confuses you or says something that you are curious about, find a way to say it.
Whatever you feel, if you trust in your gut and find a way to say what you are feeling, your sales will increase, as you get into the real dialogue that the answers to these types of questions will bring.

**TIP: If you feel it, find a way to say it!*
By David Sandler, Sandler Selling Systems

Most prospects will be refreshed with your honesty and find a way to **help** you keep the sale.

There is nothing to remember in this selling method, just be yourself, be honest and if you feel it, use that.

In communication, your goal is always an adult- adult conversation. How you achieve that is always saying what you feel. Soften with soft people and hit the tough people with it hard, mirror each of them. Tough people like and respect tough people. The same goes for softer style folks. Just mirror them and look at the diagram:

This is called the "Pendulum Theory of Communication", to have an adult-adult conversation, your goal is to always stay farther on the negative (Not OK) than the positive (OK).

12: No/Never buy, abrupt.
11: Takes phone calls when you are there, obnoxious, don't want you here, rude
10: Defending competition
9: Shuts you off
8: Fidgeting, inattentive, and occasionally listening
7: Uncomfortable
6: Neutral
5: Maybe, head nods, wishy-washy
4: Sounds good
3: Likes you
2: Enthusiastic
1: Sold/Yes

Take a look at each position on the pendulum. Where ever your prospect is on the pendulum, you stay on the negative side. If they are sold, #1, you drop down to #4, by saying "Sounds good, tell me what you mean by "wow, I've been wanting to get that from you?" A good many sold or enthusiastic prospects either have no money or no intention of ever buying. They are people pleasers who cannot say "no" to your face. These are the people that you chase with voice mails, after they tell you, "Oh, yes, I'll get it on Monday, just call me then." On the other end of the scale, say at #12, they say, "no not today, not ever from your company", you would say, "You sound upset with us, what happened, tell me about it? You would also be saying what you feel at this moment. Instead of defending your company, be empathetic and be curious about what happened. Give the upset person the space for their feelings and let them vent. Don't apologize until you have heard the whole story. Agree with them if you can, say "Well, I'm not sure that I would buy from us after that." There is no guarantee that they will ever buy and I had some of the best sales in my life after a prospect or customer started with how angry they were with us and with "no, we'll never buy from you.

Be aware of where people start out on the pendulum of communication. Remember, your job in any sales conversation, especially if you have just met the prospect, is to stay below them, you stay "less ok" than they are if they are on the positive. And on the negative side, you would carefully mirror their negative, and use what I call a take away.

TIP: Remember, opposites attract.

I once had a prospect come up to me at a cocktail reception and say "oh, you're with XXXX, we could never buy from you" and replied "how do you know that we would sell you?" He was shocked that I might not want to sell them. I could see by his reaction. His spine stiffened. He asked "how come you might not sell us?" I asked him, "Do you sell everyone" ...he replied, "No." I asked, "Peter, (looking at his name badge) why not" …. Peter replied, "Well not everyone is a good prospect for us." I said, "Well the reason we might not sell you is the same. You might not be a good fit for us." "Tell me a little bit about why you said you would never buy from us" ...and that started a dialogue that ended with me closing his business a few weeks later and it was worth over $750,000 annually and I took the business from six other suppliers of his. He consolidated all of his purchases with me despite doing business with some of those suppliers for many years, in some cases for over ten years. Why did I close that business? I left him space for his opinions and I went more negative than he did on the pendulum of communication. The only way he could swing was more positive and he did.

TIP: The Laws of Physics applies to communication, "a body in motion stays in motion", take a risk and keep the pendulum swinging.

4. Give more but don't overpromise

The days of, "Yes, we can do it all" are over. Customers don't care about the size of your company, your warehouse, the number of trucks you have, how many employees, how many factories you have or any of the other things that may give your company bragging rights.

We are not measured by what we do right but by how we deliver what we say. Do we keep our word and how do we correct issues and problems? Companies and people with integrity keep their word, no matter WHAT.

What they want is for you to deliver what you promise. If you cannot keep all the promises you make, you are over promising and out of integrity. Leave yourself room by under promising, and then really impress customers by over delivering. Give yourself room to "over deliver" by asking, "When would you like this (completed, delivered)?" If the prospects expectations are unreasonable, you could say "what if I said it will be two weeks longer than that, (you know have given yourself an additional week). If the prospect says that's ok, you have room to deliver **before** the two weeks is up. If the prospect stands firm on their original request and you know you cannot meet that date, you could say, what would happen if we missed that date? How would you feel? Let them talk. You want to help **them** hear that another week or two is not that critical and most times it's not. If it's still critical for the prospect to meet that delivery date and you cannot meet it, then you end it. You could say, "I want you to have the XXXX on time and I could not promise that. Would you like me to refer another company or do you have one in mind? Here, by allowing the prospect the space to go to a competitor and by offering to help them find another supplier, you build trust and respect that may reopen this door to a sale now or one in the future.

TIP: Under promise and over deliver.

IF you are keeping your word everywhere in your life, then you have Integrity. Notice if and when you break your word. Ask your significant other and friends if they see you as someone who keeps their word. They will tell you if you invite them to and share up front that it is better for you if they tell you the truth. You can only change, if you learn, what it is that you do not know about yourself.

There is what we know about ourselves, what we know that we don't know and what we don't know, that we don't know. I work with students and myself on learning "what I don't know, that I don't know. That is where true growth and continued success will manifest from.

5. Make relationship, stand in their shoes and get to know them better

If your first thought on every order or presentation is commission, you will see dollars shrink over time and much slower growth in commission dollars than your counterparts who think "customers." By staying in the frame of mind that you are there to "help people buy the best solution, even if it's not you", you will grow your sales faster than those sales people who focus only on their commissions. For your existing customers, do the little things: Stay with them on an issue with another department in your company until it is resolved, fix annoying balances that linger on erroneous statements; make that return the customers keeps asking about, care enough to resolve issues that are "someone else's responsibility. Once someone becomes your customer, make them your responsibility, even if the company assigns another department to do the daily service. Take care of your customer's business and your commissions will grow, especially through referrals from happy customers. **Jeffrey Gittomer author of "The Little Red Book of Selling says "If you make a sale, you can earn a commission. If you make a friend, you can earn a fortune."** Thinking "customer first, before commission, will take you to the bank more often.

TIP: People buy from people they like and trust…. can you be trusted?

"Get to know them better if you stand in their shoes"

You are first and foremost selling yourself. First impressions are the lasting ones. What is it that you want to portray to the prospects in the first few minutes? People buy from people they like and trust. Your job is to make the prospect comfortable with you. This is where bonding and appearance comes in. Let's start with the bond.

Bonding is one of the keys to sales. In my almost 30 years of coaching, managing and training sales people the biggest mistake they made was in the bond. Even though we hear about bonding all the time, many salespeople are unaware that it is how they show up that is their block to selling more. Remember, selling is about them, the prospect, not us.

A. Match and mirror the prospect, stand in their shoes…. Begin with body language first. Body language is 55% of the communication pie. Wait for the prospect to begin speaking and match their general posture. Do not play "Simon says" with the prospect. If the prospect is generally relaxed, match it. If they are sitting straight up, match it. This helps you because as you match someone, you get to feel what they are feeling in that same posture and it tells the other person's subconscious that you are like them. Your job is to help people find the right solution and to make them feel at ease with you as soon as possible. Who better to trust than someone who is helping them buy and who is more like them than not.

B. Match their tone and speed of their speech. If they talk soft and slow (usually together), match it. If they talk loud and fast, pick up your pace and volume. Tonality is 38% of the communication pie.

C. Match their need for bonding. This is most important. If you meet with someone and they want to get right to business and resist your attempts to bond, **GET RIGHT TO BUSINESS. Be direct if they are direct…. they will like that because it**

sends a message to their brain "hey, this person is just like me" "Just follow the prospects lead, go with the flow. For someone who wants to spend time with you on the bond, allot no more than 20% of the total time set aside for the appointment for the bond. Of a 60-minute call, allow for 12 minutes for bonding.

D. Thoughts have power. They are energy. Scientists have proven this. Think good thoughts. This sends good energy out from you. You can silently wish your prospect "joy, success and happiness." Deepak Chopra in his book the Seven Spiritual Laws of Success, say wishing someone "joy, success and happiness" is akin to bringing someone a gift who has invited you to their home. Hopefully, when invited to someone's home you would bring a gift, but Deepak says that if you did forget, this wish would be just like bringing them an actual gift. Imagine the power of doing this with your prospects.

E. Appearance is critical. Even though the work world has become more relaxed, appearance is critical for successful selling. As far as dress goes, dress professionally. Use common sense and remember the image you want to portray. Matching works here as well. Match the prospect's dress code. When you are setting the appointment ask "what is the dress code at your office"?

What is your dress code saying to the prospect about you and your company? Sloppy dress, sloppy company? Sloppy dress says you have no confidence in your sales ability. The same goes for provocative dress. Dressed professionally, what does that say about you and your company? The same goes with personal hygiene. How do your teeth look? How about your hair? Do you have dandruff? I once coached a guy to wear light sport coats, and or light plaids to hide his skin condition. He was a wearing blue and dark sport coat and his shoulders and neck looked like a ski resort. You are the first contact with your company that any prospect has. Think about that before you go in.

F. Are you a person of integrity? Do you keep your commitments? Are you on time? Do you return phone calls in a timely fashion? Do you fulfil your promises? Trust is built on integrity. Keep your word everywhere and sell more. It will build trust and help you bond.

G. Forget about that old axiom, "look around the prospects office to find something to bond about." You can use it if you wish, but prospects are aware of this tactic. Be yourself. I am curious about a person's background so I ask about their background in the company and sometimes I ask if they got recruited in. "Tell me about your history in this company, did you get recruited in?" That is a subtle pat on the back, a stroke. People are stroke deprived. Most people in top-level management (I hope you are calling on top management) do not get enough strokes. If they were recruited, they usually tell me all about where they came from, and if not, I ask, "If they started in the company mailroom or at the "bottom" they usually relish in telling me the history as well. It is what I am interested in and that is what I start with. I am naturally curious about people and their careers and how they succeed. Start with an interest of yours, be real, and be curious. If you do see a lot of paraphernalia around the office, ask about it, even if you are not a fan, if you are curious, ask. Remember, you do not need a "tacky tactic" if you are being real.

A word of caution though, I once noticed a lot of golf awards in the office of my prospect on a first visit. I said, "Wow, you sure are a great golfer…three holes in ones"? He replied, "I can't stand golf…." I said, "What about all the awards?" He replied… "It's not my office, we know salespeople use this stuff to try and bond so we switch offices here all the time when we have a salesperson come in for a first visit." Beware and ask first… "Is this your office?"

H. Once you ask that question, ("Tell me about your history in this company, did you get recruited in?"), watch what happens. People love to talk about themselves. After a while, with some follow up questions like, "What are your responsibilities? You can return to selling by asking the prospect, "How can we help you with those responsibilities?

I. Take notes. Ask permission first. Another stroke. May I take a few notes? Ask this after they have started sharing what is going on in the company. After you have gathered enough information about their situation, review what they have told you and validate it. It would sound like this. "May I review what you have just told me to be sure I have got it right? Review and tell them "this is typically what we are hearing from our customers" (validation by the way). Ask if you missed anything. Ask if they would like to add anything. Then ask "How do you see an outside company helping you with these issues? Listen closely, they will tell you how to sell them.

J. Take the pressure off. Tell them that you are there to help them find the right solution, even if it isn't you. Ask them if they are ok telling you that you are not the right fit for them. Tell them that you are ok with "no." This is taking the pressure off of both of you. It is reminding you that that is why you are there. To see if it is a fit for both of you. Then you could day " f I sense that your company is not a fit for us, would you mind if I say that?" After all, we do not sell everyone.

TIP: Make bonding a technique of yours, not a manipulative tactic. Practice being fully present in all your conversations.

6. Detach from outcomes

TIP: Selling becomes easier when you go with the flow.

Detaching from outcomes helps you relax in the middle of the action. How can you lose what you don't have? Being detached from outcomes, you can help people buy and be comfortable. Being detached will help you take risks with evasive buyers. How can you take a huge risk if you are attached and worried about not getting the sale?

**TIP: You can't lose what you don't have.*

Remember, you don't have it. Take a risk. I spent many years attempting to control other people and thankfully realized what a waste of energy it was.

"After you learn to detach, relax and go with the flow, life works better everywhere"

Being detached from outcomes helps you with rejection. How can you be rejected anytime if you are not attached to the outcome? View everything as just an event, not good or bad, just outcomes. Since you cannot control outcomes in life, only yourself, focus on what you can control. YOU!

When you sense things aren't going where you wanted, don't push too hard, unless you are in front of a hard driving person. Let the customer know you can see that you've missed something, then ask directly: "What did I miss? How can we get back on track?" Watch for the tell-tale signs that you have upset someone. Notice body language. Is the prospect closing up? Is he/she moving away from you, pursing lips, furrowing their brow or worse, crossing their arms and moving away from you at the same time? Anything that you sense, even a feeling that you have said something that upset them, find a way to say what you feel or see. Be prepared to soften the question first. People love to help people, so struggle on purpose if you have to. If you are feeling uncomfortable, share that. You could say, "I am feeling like you are upset, I could be wrong, tell me are you uncomfortable with this purchase, or with me?" Give them a chance to respond. Whatever it is! It could even be, "Well, I get the sense that we are not a fit? Are you feeling the same way?

**TIP: Take a few deep breaths before the call or during
to help you detach or just note your breathing.*

Your goal is to help people buy. Some prospects buy because of force. They are tired of pestering. They do anything to get away from the constant barrage of phone calls and emails. These prospects do not stay customers for long. Often, they change their mind within 24 hours and cancel orders. Have you had, what you thought was an enthusiastic prospect, say that "things really looked good" and yet they did not return your calls? Even after they said, "call me on Monday and I'll give you an order." It could be because you put too much pressure on them and you did not realize it. If this was the case, the prospect just wanted to be rid of you. They do not return calls. Do your research on this. Customers, given respect and the space to buy what fits, will stay your customers.

You waste energy pushing a customer who is a "soft personality" type, when they have decided it's a "no sale." It's your fault you missed something - use the energy instead to discover what you have missed or, to move on to a new customer. Do the both of you a favour and voluntarily close a presentation that is going nowhere. Many times, recognizing the ending actually opens real dialogue that might get a sale. So, go with the flow. You are easier to be around and you will attract new outcomes.

The only exception to the above is when you are dealing with HARD DRIVING personality types…. you must match and mirror them … give them what they give you…. push them, prod them…give them back what they give you just as hard or harder…they will like and respect you for it.

7. Don't Settle for Less

**TIP: You are always harvesting something you planted,
if you want a bigger harvest…. Plant more!*

Don't cave in to the Income Avalanche. With fear that you won't have enough income, you make poor decisions on business prospects, accepting customers who drain energy. Doing business with inappropriate types of people doesn't work. While you are running around meeting the demands of these customers, who you have trained to take advantage of you, you could be working with people who will allow you to make an abundant living. If you haven't helped customers grow, then do so now. Make them more profitable. Maybe you could gradually raise their prices. Educate them on what makes your company more productive and hence more competitive. **Train** them to prosper too.

I remade my whole territory one year by asking myself "who would you call on, who would you sell if you did not worry about money?

If you'd do something different, then you could make the change. If you said, like I did, "I have the greatest job in the world, and…. I'd change this or that" - then write down the changes. See how you can live into them, then give yourself a timetable to make the changes happen.

I used this plan to remake my own territory and followed with **two** record setting years and "Salesperson of the Year" award.

Starting with the end in mind, I thought about what needed improving in my territory. I wanted to deal with larger customers and make 100% more than I was making and have more time to myself to enjoy life. Next I reviewed each customer and ranked them by sales, profit, commission and the time they required from me. I noticed that many of the low margin customers took a lot of my time. I also noticed that some of the large customers required that I showed up each week. I knew that to get more time to see new, larger customers or to increase sales in my best customers, I would have to re-arrange the time I was spending and increase the margins on many of my existing customers.

Next I targeted those customers that had the potential to grow and those that needed a reduced call schedule and higher margins.

I set meetings with each client and told them upfront that I and my company wanted me to increase sales by 20% or more during the next 12 months. I then told them of my new plans. If it involved calling on them in person only once per month, instead of weekly, we discussed it. I asked how they felt, and together we settled on how we would make it work. I set phone calls in between, or trained some of their staff to place the orders, etc.

Price is not why people buy

TIP: Customers will say price determines the sale and it's not true. You determine if you get your price or not.

Get your price. Here is how:

1. Start upfront with prospects by setting the expectation.... I would always say, "we are not the lowest price...we focus on good service and results and would you agree that we usually get what we pay for in life?" or "How do you price your products? Are you the lowest price provider in your business?" Usually their answer here was "no", and I would add, "Well, neither are we." If they did answer yes then perhaps they would not be a fit for me and I would ask more questions to determine a fit like "is price the only factor you use when deciding on a purchase like this?", etc.

2. Starting with the end in mind, what is the ideal margin you require to provide your customer with the level of service they expect and that aligns with your mission statement? Do the research. Where are your company's products or services priced in relation to your competition? If you are the lowest or close why not go up 5%? Raise prices on all services and items that your customers buy because you have it...or that you sell very few of each month...by 10%. They are buying because you have it or you are very good at it. What is your market share? If it's below 2% or above 30% you could raise pricing. If you are on the lower share of the market, you can raise prices because lowering 5% will not raise your market share significantly and could put you out of business. Hopefully your service or your mission justifies the increase. If you are on the higher end of market share, determine why you have achieved that proportion of share? Perhaps you have the reputation for great service and can justify a 2 – 5% higher margin. Test it, have your marketing staff do the survey or hire someone to do it. If they justify the increase, you can get a quick return on that investment.

Pay full price when you shop. Be willing to pay a merchant you like top dollar, or for a service, again from a merchant who earns your trust and respect. What we give we get in life, so if you want full price, be willing to pay it. I have worked with sales people who complain about customers or prospects being focused only on price and when I inquire about how they buy something or ask them to tell me about the last time they bought a car, they often have quite a story about how they really "worked the sales person" and got a really good deal. Are you always bragging about how you got a low price?

*TIP: If price is the only reason people buy from you,
look at how you buy things…. practice paying full price yourself.*

3. Use Intention. Albert Einstein once said, "80% of the movement of matter is intention." Intend that you will make your margin. Use affirmations to reinforce your intention. A good affirmation is "I am trusted, I give great service and I am paid full price." Get Wayne Dyers book, "The Power of Intention." Use your imagination. Visualize contracts signed and handshakes with those margins agreed upon. See the happy faces of your prospects. Feel what it would feel like to have outcomes like these. Use the power of your thoughts to help you create the world you envision.

*TIP: Use your imagination, see yourself
succeeding beyond your wildest dreams.*

4. Be prepared to say no if the price the prospect is attempting to negotiate is below your margin bottom line. Real negotiations usually begin at no. You could say "that price does not work for me, (pause) …….it would mean we would have to cut our service somewhere. I could cut somewhere in the proposal…. what would be ok to cut back on?" Walk from it if you have to. Prospects respect your boundaries and if they do not, you do not need them. Many times, I have held my line on pricing and walked, only to have the prospect either hold me from leaving or call me up a day or so later to say, "I have a purchase order for you, would you come in to discuss the final details?"

5. Read the book "Blue Ocean Strategy" …create a Blue Ocean Strategy for your company and get your margins without hesitation because you are serving a market that has customers calling you for your expertise. Not because you are another "me too", selling the same product or service and price becomes the major determining factor.

6. If you decide to operate in the low-price arena, get your operation lean, mean, efficient and productive and give great service and low pricing and make a profit at the same time.

Your market, your territory is what you have made it You can remake your company or your territory anytime you like. Here's how:

1. Start with the end in mind, as Stephen Covey says, Set your annual income goal.

2. What is the average sale for the territory? How many customers or sales are required to hit the goal? What if the average sale doubled? What kind of prospects or customers fit the profile of doubling the average sale? How many of the existing customers fit the profile of the increased average sale? Make a list of the existing customers that do not fit your new profile. Determine which customers have the potential to fit your new profile over time. Perhaps they are buying from some of your competitors and you could increase your business or they are growing or have plans for expansion. Any customers that will not fit your new plan, give them to someone else in the company, perhaps a trainee or decide to make the phone the only way that you will be in contact with them the majority of the time. You could raise their prices and just see what happens.

3. Next, using your new picture of the new, ideal customer for you…make a list of target accounts. Ask your existing customers if they know anyone who works at these accounts and would they recommend you? Would they introduce you to them? Even if the person they know is not the decision maker, their friend or contact would probably know the decision maker or know someone at the company who does. Either way, you get to make a *warm call, instead of a cold call.* Next, for targets that you cannot get introduced into…develop a marketing post card, something that would get their attention concerning your product or service. Perhaps you know of a particular problem or pain that many of your customers had before you sold them. Send the post card to the target accounts (mail 20 or 25 at a time, it's easier to follow up on a small amount, remember to keep it manageable) Mail them three or four times….and be sure to include the

following message on the third and fourth card, "I will be calling you to ask for an appointment next week." More on warming up a call, in chapter 12.

Now make sure that you call. Your goal is to keep the mailing going with new targets so that eventually you will be calling 20 to 25 targets per week, 4 or 5 per day... manageable. Your job is action. Keep the action up and sales will increase.

TIP: Sales behaviour is planting seeds of a future harvest.

4. Cold calls. If you are going to cold call, make them outrageous. The targets should be the best of the best. Start at the top. Call the president. Who calls her or him anyway? Very few people start at the top. Call on prospects that you have previously thought would never buy from you. Even the ones that you think, in your mind that the competition has "sewn up." If you only make one of these calls per day that equals five per week and over 50 weeks that is 250 calls per year...if you only get 20 appointments and close 5, you are closing 5 of your targets from the list of the "best of the best" customers, that buy what you sell. Imagine the impact of that one activity on your sales results? Imagine the impact on your income. Feel how it would feel. How would your company feel about you? Feel it. It is behaviour that gets results over time, you keep working and forget about outcomes.... If you are working each day and working on yourself as well, the outcomes will be positive.

8. Develop a System to follow

Prospects have been using a system designed as a defensive measure against high pressure and non-professional salespeople.

Does this sound familiar? Prospects tell you that they are very interested and ask you to tell them all about your company and what you sell. You tell them and ask for the order. They start to work you on price or ask you to do a quote or formal proposal. You do one and again ask for the order. They tell you it looks good and ask you to call back in a week or so. You do and you get stuck in what I call voice mail jail.

Prospects are either using you to get a better price from their current supplier or service provider or they are getting free consulting.

I suggest that you could use a system to help you determine if prospects are really committed to what you provide. Then you could decide to move forward or not. And you will be helping them make the same decision as well. Help them buy.

You could use my suggested system that follows or develop one of your own. Remember that your prospects are using one, so be prepared.

First; Bond.
Set aside 20% of the allotted time for the call to bond, except if the client shows no inclination to bond.

Second; Set the rules of the call.
An outline or agenda. Tell them "to help make our time together productive you have an agenda; would they mind if you went over it?" Tell them that you will have to ask what might seem like a lot of questions to help them determine if you are the right company for them. Give them permission to ask you questions as well. Tell them that in your experience that most people ask a lot of questions as well and some of them are… (Suggest some questions, ones that you would like them to ask!).

Third; Provide pressure relief.
Then say, "If at any point, you feel like my company is not a good fit, do you mind telling me "no, it's not going to work", I'm ok with no. After they respond, you could also add, "on the other hand, we do not do business with everyone, would you mind if I came to the same conclusion if I said that "gee, I get a feeling that you are not a fit for us, do you mind if I share why? (This could pave the way to reopen the sale).

Fourth. Use the 70/30 rules
Use the 70/ 30 to gauge commitment. What you are feeling, find a way to say it. Bring up your biggest fears.

Prepare questions that will encourage the prospect to talk 70% of the time. Listen and take notes to gauge for areas of pain or concern. Listen for problems that are potentially costing them lots of money if they do not fix them. Listen for problems that could cost them their job, company, or prestige if they ignore them. Listen for a desire to have a new future, unlike the past. Ask about the past, how long have they had the problem? What have they done to fix it? Has it worked? Have they told their existing supplier? What happened?

If the responses have them telling you a story of woe, ask them how they feel about that? Whatever you feel, during their responses, find a way to say it and whatever your biggest fear is, bring it up.

This builds an adult – adult relationship. People will respect you for it. Refer to the communication chart in Key 9.

Fifth; Determine budget.

Ask in general terms what have they set aside to fix the problem? If they respond with "we never share that" ask "If I said it was going to cost between X and X, are you in that range? Closer to X? (Lower x).

TIP: The lower x should be higher than your lowest price.

Six; Decision, ask about the decision.

Ask "the last time you made a decision like this, what d d that process look like? Will you be bringing anyone else in to help you? (If yes, ask if they are there now, or when will they be including them in a meeting.) Suggest that typically, you attend the final decision meeting to help them all make the best decision for their business. Ask how do they see you helping them make the decision?

Seven; Present

Present only to the needs expressed during the questioning, nothing more, and nothing less. Before you start, ask if you can go over your notes to be sure you have all of their concerns correct. Go over the list and validate their concerns, "We see this...) Ask if they have anything to add, then ask which of the ones you went over would be number 1 if they rated them and 2 and so on to three. You only need the top three to start your presentation. Start with the top three.

Eight; Close.

Take the temperature first. Ask "on a scale of 0 to 10, if 0 was, we would not go to the next step and 8 was we would go to the next step, where are you on that scale? If over five, ask, what would you need to hear to go to 8? If they are below 5 ask "what would you need to hear to get to a 5? If they are at 8, simply ask, "What would you like to do next? They will tell you how to close them.

If they are at 0.... you could say… "Oh, I must have missed something, where did you feel that we were not a fit?" Listen intently as you could reopen and it could be the time to end it as well.

Nine; Set the deal.

Be sure the deal is set. Once you close, hand the purchase order or deposit check back to the prospect before you go and ask, "Sometimes, not very often, and probably not the case here, people change their minds for various reasons after I leave, is there anything else you think we need to cover before I take your (check or Po)? This gives the prospect the chance to deal with buyer's remorse before you go. Did you ever leave a store thinking, "why did I buy that?" Discover if your prospects are feeling and remorse over their decision and help them with it. If you are detached from outcomes, you can bring this up easily and prospects will thank you for it.

Remember during the whole interview, whatever you feel, whatever you fear, pay attention to it. Find a way to say it.

Ten;
Keep track of your results.

*TIP: You cannot manage what you do not measure.

Track how you are doing and use a system, this one or another but using a system can help you figure out what you may be doing wrong, but only if you track your results.

9. Sales are flat and or feeling stuck, what to do?

Everyone hits the wall sometimes...everyone.

The first thing to do is admit that your own behaviour the last six months or year has been below par. In a Cause and Effect world, you created this...accepting responsibility is critical. You could say, "Steve, I lost a big account...they went out of business how is that my fault or how did I create that?"

My reply... "you did not work on enough new business to account for any potential loss." And "always be aware of any potential threats." "That's your job."

Now that we've got that over with...let's focus on the solution. And speaking of focus, what have you been focusing on in the past year? What has most of your thinking been about? Did you only see challenges? Did you convince yourself "times are tough, there is a lot of competition? Negative thinking eventually brings negative results. What was your time spent on? Did you slack or invest your time in the wrong areas? Are you calling on VITO's? (Very Important Top Officers).
When I work with teams or individuals whose sales have been flat typically I find that it's a combination of mental and physical reasons. Mental being a lowered expectation and settling for less and not challenging themselves to reach higher and have fun doing it. Sometimes too, it's personal reasons...a life change like divorce or a health challenge in the family or their own... and or a physical challenge like low energy or depression... (mental and physical).

If it is depression, get help...if not, I can help.

Think low tide and high tide...Perhaps the tide is out...it always returns...when you change things will change. Begin a mental routine every morning of super charging your energy. Hit the gym...meditate on a favourite passage from an author who inspires you. Spend time in quiet, meditating on the results you are intending. See yourself succeeding. Picture deals being made and contracts written. See yourself shaking hands...picture mentally the success beforehand. Study successful people in sales. Model your behaviour after those successful people. Speak with successful sales people you work with...and begin to act as if you already have that success.

If you have been in a rut, perhaps the energy level that you have been projecting out into the world and in meetings has been low or negative. When you are going in to a call or picking up the phone, think of all the pictures you have in your mind from your visualizing sessions. You can only control you...raise the energy you project by silently wishing others around you, success, joy and happiness. Include those you call on too...wish them silently the same. Begin to make a difference in the lives of everyone around you. Acknowledge and praise people you work with and people in stores that you shop and even fireman and policeman and woman. I say "I am grateful for the work that you do, thank you...I couldn't do it...thank you." It's amazing the shift in anyone's body language when you praise them...you get to see the effect of your cause. It enlivens me every time acknowledge and or praise others... I have heard Joel Osteen say, "when you complain, you remain, when you praise you will be raised."

Speaking of complaining...do you complain or whine a lot? That is also a low energy activity and does not return good to you...unless you complain to someone with a suggestion to fix a problem...to those who can fix it...now that is positive and sounds like this... "hey our software has been doing xxxx and I suggest that we address it by doing xxxxx? What do you think? What are your ideas?" Now you are having a dialogue about fixing something with a suggestion to help. That is positive. Too often, people complain with no suggestion to fix anything and they complain to those co-workers who are not the ones who can fix it. That is leaving everyone around you sapped of energy and it marks you as a low energy complainer. Whining is not attractive at all...telling others how difficult your life is...is a dumb waste of energy and if you whine in front of customers or co-workers, you look dumb. Catch yourself doing it and stop...

Are you a gossip? I have worked with owners of companies who gossiped and made fun of employees behind their backs. It told me that this person would gossip about me when I wasn't around...and these types of people always do because they have a very low self-image and they have to lower others to feel good about themselves. If you are a gossip, quit it...it says you have very low energy and self-esteem. IS that the energy of a winner?

Get a coach, one that will kick your butt...get you to do things that sound uncomfortable and should be. If you are not making yourself uncomfortable then how can you have a new future...one unlike the past? If you keep doing what you're doing and expecting a different result that is Einstein's definition of insanity. How can doing the same old thing bring anything new?

The biggest impact action is managing the energy you project onto the world. When you change, things will change.

Study the chapter in this book about living in a Universe. You are a part of a miracle and how it works is described in detail. Get out there and start giving what you want to get. Help others and you will get help. Get out of your stuck head and by being in action, things will begin to happen. Think of it as planting new seeds. Give it time...

Section 2 "Seeds of Success"

"We are always harvesting something we planted"
                                                                    Steve Lentini

10. Use and understand the "Seasons"

Use the examples that Nature provides all around us for free; Nature provides us with a powerful example of how to have an abundant harvest. In nature, we see four distinct seasons. Spring, Summer, Fall and Winter.

In Spring the farmer prepares the ground for the planting of the seeds. The salesperson in spring is preparing the ground for his/her future success. How does a salesperson prepare the ground? Make meeting new people every day your goal, not selling them. Your purpose in spring is to prepare the ground and to plant the seeds. Resist the urge to "rush the harvest." Too often, salespeople attempt selling, or harvesting, the first time they call or meet someone. Prospects usually "pull back" from early attempts to "harvest" or sell. They feel the pressure. Would you stand over a tomato seedling and shout, "ok now, give me a tomato"? Of course, not. We understand the cycles in nature much better than we do with people and yet the laws are the same. Prepare the ground, plant the seed and then wait. The same goes for selling. Prepare the ground with research about where your ideal customers hang out. Then plant seeds by meeting them there, where they hang out. You can also prepare the ground with effective marketing mailing and advertising campaigns. Good Public relations and community work also helps, especially when your efforts get noticed and published in the newspapers or in the media.

*TIP: You are always getting what you are giving: GIVE MORE!

Do the research and prepare the ground. Then plant seeds by meeting people and making relationships first. Find out how you can help people. Discipline your thoughts and judgments when you first meet people. Think only good thoughts, I silently salute the "Divinity" in each person I meet every day and I send them my blessings as a gift" or I wish them "joy, success and happiness." Thoughts have energy, so sending positive thoughts to your prospects, clients, friends and relatives couldn't hurt......? Think of the times that you have called someone and noticed that they did not seem ok. How did you notice? You felt that their energy was lowered or heard something in their voice that said things weren't right. Customers and prospects will pick up on the energy that you are sending when you are thinking positive thoughts about them.

After the seeds sprout in spring, next comes the summer.

Think care, nurture, feed and weed

Summer is a time for care of the crop. The seeds of spring have broken through the hard ground. Now is the time for consistent effort. Care for your customers. Little time off and diligence is required. Protection of the crops, nurturing, feeding, weeding are the daily routines to provide for the growth into strong plants or customers that will give the bountiful harvest. Again, you will face many tests as nature deems you fit or not for the upcoming harvest. "Will you rail against the storms, rocks, bugs and weeds?" as Jim Rohn says in his book "The Garden of Life." Call them unfair and unjust? If so, you are classified as one who seeks the reward without the effort, something in return for nothing. In our Cause and Effect Universe, this cannot be. If you expect something for nothing you will reap just that. It is not unfair; it is just how it is. The Universe does not weep for your failure or celebrate your victory. If after planting your seeds, you do not see results, the lesson here is to persist through the doubt. Keep your vision. Take some time daily to visualize your goals. Imagine contracts being signed and checks coming to you. I spend time daily actually "seeing" the checks, using my imagination. –I imagine the check. In my mind's eye, I see "Pay to the order of" .... And the amounts made out.... then the written amount and the check signed.... I see "handshake deals and contracts signed."

Expect to be tested. You are tested as humans grow strong by facing obstacles and difficulty. Gratitude and action is required for all of our adversity. For our character grows with adversity and in our response to it, not with inaction. As we come to expect difficulty, we can celebrate our future strength and see, that in the absence of adversity, we would wither and be blown away with the first "storms of our lives."

*TIP: Remember "Diamonds are made with a
combination of extreme pressure and abrasion."*

I heard a story about the "Biosphere" in Colorado. When it first opened, under a dome was a grand experiment. Scientists were duplicating everything in nature, under a dome to observe all the cycles of life for possible life on far away planets. The idea was that, if it worked, we could duplicate our life on barren planets, under a controlled environment like the dome. Scientists noticed the trees that were planted, would fall over when they reached between five and six feet tall. They were scrawny and not very healthy looking. They tried different foods, tested the soils, varied the temperatures and the light conditions but nothing worked. Then, one day someone realized what had been missing. Wind! Varied winds, especially strong winds, served to break some of the roots as the trees swayed back and forth in response. Where the roots broke, new shoots formed which went deeper into the ground, serving to further anchor the tree to protect it from future high winds and storms. So, to, storms and the high winds of our lives allow us to form more and deeper roots. With this new appreciation for our storms we can be in gratitude when they come. We can know deep down that we are being prepared and strengthened for a future bountiful harvest. What a gift.

*TIP: Care for your customers give them the service they deserve.
Feed and weed, watch out for pests (competitors)
who would take your harvest? Pay attention.*

Next, the harvest

The long-anticipated return for what we have sown. What we have now in our lives is our harvest from our previous spring. Whatever our preparation was, whatever seeds we planted we are now reaping. If you are frustrated, unhappy, broke, unemployed or deeply in debt, you have planted the seeds of this yourself. Accept the responsibility and move on.

You could blame others for your harvest, but if you planted a garden and it withered and died or if you neglected it and the harvest was meagre, would you blame it on your employer, your parents, your spouse, your business partners, or any others? Of course, not, and yet we see humans attempt to do this with their lives all the time. Until we let go of the "blame game", the victim, pity mode we cannot advance to a rich and bountiful harvest. The harvest is a time to let go of things.

*TIP: "If you don't like your experience of the world,
change how the world is experiencing you."* Steve Lentini

Just as the trees let go of the leaves. Just as the blossoms and fruits fall away, we too must decide now what and who to let go of in our lives. To have a new future and new harvest we must decide to let go of old patterns and choices that have held us to this harvest of gloom. And yet this is also a reason to celebrate. Because whatever our current harvests, we can begin to plant anew.

Winter, don't forget to rest

Winter is our time to rest, to surrender. Surrender to the idea that things are still happening underground, although we cannot see them. Before planting anew, after any harvest, a time of reflection is required. Learning is a good thing too in winter. A time for seminars, classes and study of what could be next. Meditation about what did not work in the last harvest, what did and preparation and planning for the next planting too. Winter is a good time for journaling. Writing down what the recent harvest brought in to the storehouse or the lack of it. Tying the resultant harvest back to the activities and action we took in spring. Notice any patterns of self-doubt and defeat. Look for the "blame game" and victim dialogue within yourself. Even if you have just had a bountiful harvest, one cannot assume that this pattern will repeat. You must take the same care with planting the next crop, selecting the site, soil and seeds carefully so as to ensure another bountiful harvest.

We humans are built to grow, expand and produce. We are happiest when we are risking and reaching deep down within ourselves using all of our gifts. Magnanimity is joyful. Pusillanimity is not. Pusillanimity is holding back one's gifts. The Universe knows that you are holding out. Dare and dream big. Believe. Now is the time to prepare for the time when the earth warms and the soil loosens. Getting ready for the slip and slide from the mud of spring, the high winds and the rains.

Preparation now will make winters enjoyable as you will see the need for winter in your cycle. You will understand winters role and be grateful for it. Unlike our western society, where rest is scorned, you will come to value it as you rest and prepare for the next planting while others are still running around wondering what the hell just happened in the last harvest. Not even aware that the cycles and seasons of nature are here to teach, instruct and even comfort us. Comfort us with the idea that cycles and seasons are normal and a part of our lives as well, not just something to go through or complain about each year. *

*information on the seasons comes from Toni Stone, c/o Wonder Works Studio, 401 Buck Hollow Road, Fairfax, VT, www.wonderworks.org and from Jim Rohn's book "The Seasons of Life

11. Set Time and boundaries and sell only the best of the best.

Set your goals high enough and be strong enough to eliminate time-wasting customers and prospects from your list. Train customers to respect your time. Your time is too valuable to waste on people who lack the respect you need. You need the time to respond to your good customers and good targets. Thinking like a lawyer or an accountant can help. Both track their time and charge by the minute. When you are in front of a customer or answering an "urgent" call from a client set the clock and measure the financial return you are getting for the time invested. The customer at the bottom of your list needs a boost or perhaps you can start a junior salesperson on his or her way in your company. This does not mean that you "rush" prospects or customers. You cannot manage what you do not measure. So be aware of people who are time wasters. You can assign inside sales to help with smaller customers, offer them to your boss and ask for his or her advice, (the boss will love that you are focusing on being more productive).

Setting priorities help you establish boundaries around what you are willing to spend time on and with whom. Once you have established boundaries, you can say no to the prospects, customers, and situations that do not fit with the established priorities. Many sales and business people who are mired in a rut or not as successful as they wish just cannot say no or are people pleasers. People pleasers lack the self-respect to set boundaries. I speak with business owners whose main lament is that they have experienced salespeople that have hit a plateau and have been stuck at or near the same sales levels for many years. When confronted with their mediocrity, they defend themselves with excuses like, "well, if there weren't so many backorders, or the competition is killing us." "The installers are always late" or "The programmers never deliver the new upgrade on time." Whatever the excuse that is just what it is, an excuse. They cannot see that they are the block and the main reason for the sales plateau.

If you are one of the above, step back and look at all the excuses that have held you back. Stop wasting time pleasing customers, stop doing busy work to excuse yourself from making new calls, joining an association of your peers, networking or any other productive work.

Setting boundaries and saying no will be uncomfortable at first. Practice with low risk scenario's and people. Notice how you feel the first time you say no. Your self-respect will increase. Then as you increase your free time be sure to invest *it wisely.* Time is a salespersons inventory. Manage it wisely by setting priorities and boundaries.

TIP: Read "The Power of a Positive No" by William Ury.

We NEVER have to settle for less than the best of the best.

How do we get the best of the best, you ask?

1. Start with the end in mind. What is the ideal prospect or customer for your business? Who is the ideal? What makes your company the best of the best to serve their market? Do whatever it takes, spend whatever time or money and set your company up to serve the best of the best if you are not suited to serve that market now. Why would the best of the best buy from you? Understanding who your ideal customer is and how you are the best at serving them helps you prepare questions that will determine if they are a fit for you and you for them. You are doing both of you a favour by uncovering what is the ideal supplier or company to serve their needs. How can you walk away if you are uncertain what will absolutely NOT work for you?

2. Be certain about when to walk away. Certainty is not only necessary it is absolute here. You cannot waiver on this. You could decide to set up a trial if you are feeling like a prospect could be a fit, a trial with the upfront understanding that you are trying them out... that you are uncertain if you are the best fit for them. Explain upfront in the call, that you are going to ask a lot of questions because you are there to help them find the best fit, NOT TO SELL THEM ANYTHING. Tell them you are there to help them buy the best solution, even if it is not you. You could also tell them that you do not sell everyone and ask; "is it ok with you if, at some point, I feel that we are not a fit for each other, that I tell you?"

      Buyers today are very sophisticated. Chances are they have already done a lot of research about their choices in the market, before they invited you in. The old days of selling are over... people buy from people they like and trust and you build trust by being open and honest. People are relieved when you help them buy, and if they do not buy from you today, they will tomorrow or they will refer you. I have often consulted software companies and their customer's biggest complaint are that they lie about everything... delivery dates, the cost of writing extras to the program, service times... everything. Imagine their reaction to a salesperson that told them upfront things like "we are not the best at delivery times... sometimes we take over six months to deliver special fixes to the software... how do you feel about that?" Most of the competitors are lying saying things like..." Oh, we get the extras written in no time... just a few days...." ... My clients tell the truth and their sales explode... who doesn't want to buy from someone who is honest?

      *TIP: Your goal is to look different from your competition.

3. Detach from the outcome. You will not say no to a prospect if you are tied to your goals or the bills that are due... Let it go and you will attract what you want... You won't until you do, so do it now. When you let the outcome go and say no to people who are not a fit... the Universe responds to your certainty. You will get the reputation of serving only the best of the best. I only help those who are truly dedicated to taking their "self" on. Those totally dedicated to being the best of the best, and today people pay me $2,500, $5,000, $20,000 and more to help them improve. I have clients committing to my programs for two, three and four years or more. Do you think this would be happening if I had continued to say yes to everyone?

      *TIP: Be different by being open and honest.

4. Set your price and stick to it. That will help you say no. If they say "you're too high," you can say, "well that is my price, what do we do now?" Before you go, you can ask, "What is their experience in the past when they have gone with the cheapest solution?" All you want to do here is to have them hear, in their own words, whether the lower cost provider has been the best choice in the past. It could begin a new dialogue about what your "best of the best" services would bring them. If not, you cannot lose what you did not have. Walk away. Certain, sure and assured knowing that the "best of the best" are on their way to you.

5. Spend some time each day, at the beginning or end, or both if you can, visualizing and meditating (visioning…. spend some time quietly receiving a vision on how the future will be or on what direction or decision to make) on how the best of the best customer would look and feel. See, in your imagination, large contracts, happy customers, big checks with your name on them. See you being stretched and challenged by these "best of the best" clients. Feel how it would feel to win these great clients. Feel how it would feel if you only targeted and won the best of the best. How much of the market share do you have? 1%, 2%, not even 1/10 of 1% (I bet that is the truth)? So, why are you targeting the lowest 1/10th? Why aren't you starting at the top of your market? IF YOU ARE ONLY GOING TO SERVE 1% OF YOUR MARKET TOPS, WHY ARE YOU OPERATING AT THE BOTTOM?

Try this out for two years.

Start with the end in mind; define what the best of the best looks like. Set your company up to serve the best of the best if you are not yet capable. Be certain of your new direction. Who do you prefer to buy from? Confident, assured and certain people or wishy-washy dish rags that work for anyone? Or for any amount? Set your price. Detach from outcomes and be prepared to walk away. NO, will never sound better, when it comes from you or them, if you will not budge, if you are certain. Spend quiet time seeing your goal, feeling how it will feel when it happens.

**TIP: IT WILL HAPPEN IF YOU ARE CERTAIN OF IT.*
BE PATIENT.

Remember, if you only have 1/10 of 1% of the market, which end makes the most sense to spend your resources on?

Who deserves it more?

I can't think of anyone better, can you?

12. Deal cheerfully with objections and complaints.

**TIP: "Ask yourself "what is a customer worth?"*

I believe that sales people should not deal with an objection until the prospect has had an opportunity to deal with it first. Typical sales people answer every question they are asked. If you say something that might kill the sale, the prospect will usually not share that information until you are chasing them through voice mail. Let's look at two scenarios.

Scenario 1.

Prospect: Is your machine guaranteed?

Typical Sales person: Yes, it has a one-year guarantee.

Prospect: One year? I just looked at a competitor's machine and their guarantee is two years.

Scenario 2.

Prospect: Is your machine guaranteed?

You: Yes, what type of guarantee are you looking for?

Scenario one leaves you in a box. Scenario two leaves the door open for you to try to match the prospects expectations. Try using scenario two from now on and see if it makes selling a little easier. Whatever you are asked, ask them about it. If you slow down and listen, you will remember to ask about the question rather than answer it and possibly lose their trust, make them uncomfortable and lose the sale. Reversing the question usually works very well. If someone asked you about your terms, you could say, "What kind of terms are you looking for?" "How long does it take for support staff to learn your new program? You would reverse by saying "what time frame for teaching your support staff would work for you?"

Whatever you are asked, you reverse the question to help you structure an offer that fits what the prospect wants, or it will help you understand if their expectations are unreasonable. The negotiation can begin then or you could choose to end the process. Whatever way it turns out, you are always working on the truth.

**TIP: You reverse a question because it's not important
what you think on a sales call or what you think the solution is...
it's most important to find out what the prospect thinks.*

In this Universe that we live in, physicists are now saying that creation happens in the space between things. If you are listening, without having to jump in with your remarks or defending, things can happen in the space you create by listening. By listening and leaving some silence before you speak, you are allowing the space for your customer or prospect to feel heard. When we feel, heard or listened to, we feel better. Whether you are resolving a dispute or listening to a prospect object to some part of your offering, listen and leave some silence in between your responses and allow something new to be created. Sometimes prospects will solve the objection themselves or an upset client will suggest the solution to a problem that will satisfy them.

TIP: Silence creates the space for miracles to occur.

Step back, listen and wait. Watch what happens. I work at listening every day and at leaving space for others to have their position and great things have happened and all I did was listen.

TIP: "Respond to complaints cheerfully and resolve quickly, response equals respect.

When your customers call you, make sure you respond quickly. Remember, procrastination has a cost. I have a client who is always procrastinating with his customers. He makes promises and is always late or forgets completely to deliver what he has promised. He usually ends up with gigantic problems that cost him a lot of money to fix or he has to give big discounts to keep people from being really mad at him or worse he loses the customer. Service is 80% of selling and sales. Not only does this show the customers you value their time, it also demonstrates respect and professionalism.

Remember you do not have to fix everything in that moment - don't promise too much. Give yourself time - under promise - over deliver. The customer will appreciate your quick response. By delaying your response, you usually end up with infuriated customers.

Give your customers your car phone, home phone, beeper, etc. In my 30 years of sales, few ever called me at home.

Resolve problems quickly. Remember the following:

- Expect problems
- Quick response to an angry customer
- Remember, under - promise over deliver

When you get on the road every day, expect problems. By expecting problems, you are not surprised or upset once they occur. When you are upset, you are wasting the time and energy that could be spent solving the problem. If similar problems continuously occur, bring them to the attention of management. If you are the individual running the show, get your operational staff on the job.

TIP: Life is a problem, so what…. deal with it.

But again, do expect problems on a daily basis. Even wonder what they will be. This way you will be mentally prepared to stay upbeat. You will not be defeated by any problems because you will be prepared. When a customer has a complaint, respond quickly. A quick response defuses an angry customer. By delaying your response, it usually upsets the customer even more. Remember "nothing worthwhile in life is gained by avoiding what is uncomfortable initially." ** Hit problems head on; it's never as bad as you think. Always remember to under promise and over deliver. Give yourself as much time as you can get to fix the problem - if the customer needs something right away - attend to it. Do whatever it takes. If you delay, you are making things worse.

If you do get a call from or if you call on a customer who is upset with you or your company, use the following do's and don'ts for successful dispute resolution.
** Steve Lentini

Do's
- Listen intently and take notes

Before you respond, take a moment or two and allow
silence, create space and then say something like;
- "I'm sorry to hear that"
- Use we a lot, "We apologize, we goofed", etc.
- Uh oh! We did what?
- I'm not sure I would buy from us.

Anything else?
- What can I do to fix it for you? Or what would you like us to do to fix it?
- Follow up with a written memo to customer with steps taken and cc to departments involved.
- Under Promise and over deliver here.
- Get back to the customer again
  within a week to follow up.

Don'ts
- Talk too much
- Talk over the customer

No defending, defending says you are right and they are wrong. Never make anyone wrong, they are the customer
- "I'm sorry, it will never happen again
  (how can you be sure and what if it did?)
- "We've already fixed it"
- "That darn warehouse or driver"
- Never use the word "they"

TIP: Ask yourself "what does a customer cost?",
when considering the solution to a problem or issue.

Research shows that the cost of acquiring a customer today has gone up for all industries. Depending on your industry it could be anywhere from $500 to $50,000 or more. Teach your staff and remember this when an issue arises. Wouldn't it make sense to resolve a $500 issue quickly for a customer that costs $10,000 to acquire.

DO THE MATH.

Remember to **fall back** during an exchange with an angry or upset customer. Take the hit early on. Suggest if it fits, that you might have made the mistake. Do not propose solutions; let the customer suggest how they would like it fixed. Follow up and you will keep that customer.

Just like in dealing with objections, create space here for something to happen by allowing silence. Those uncomfortable moments when no one speaks are perfect for dispute resolution as well. Silence tells the prospect that you are taking everything in that they are saying. Many times, they will offer the solution to someone who is listening and reasonable.

Bring up your biggest fears. With customers who are very upset at a repeating mistake or numerous different mistakes, I would fear losing their business. So, I started bringing up that fear. I would say after allowing them to blow off steam, "Ken, you are very upset and I agree and understand, you should be, I am a little uncomfortable right now…. (pause), I am sensing that you are so upset that this is going to get in the way of us doing business going forward?

Every time that I brought up my biggest fear, I got to answer their biggest concerns. Sometimes customers would say right then, "no, I know you are going to fix this and we are going to do business", or they would say, "No, I'm not saying that, we are still going to do business" Or sometimes they would say "well, I might go elsewhere, here are my concerns" …. At that point I listened intently, and wrote down what they said. That was the solution to continuing to do business. I never lost a customer when I brought up my biggest fear, in fact, it was only when I didn't that we lost the business. Because we left something unsaid and unresolved. By bringing up my biggest fear, we were discussing what we were both thinking anyway. We were able to discuss the solution as a result. **Their solution.**

When a customer gave their concerns, I would respond by saying, "what if we could only do 50% of what you are asking? What if 70%? What if 90% I never promised 100%, because after all, we had just made multiple mistakes, would you believe someone who made those kinds of promises. By bringing up my fear that we might only fix 50% or 70% or 90%, I knew and they heard themselves say what they would do. We both knew when I left what I had to do to ensure that I kept the business/ I made sure we did it, we delivered, and we kept the business. I also had under promised and left room for us to over deliver.

13. When Networking and Prospecting, Use Your Contacts

I once worked for a company that needed quick sales growth and the President's father had a contact in a large potential customer that we wanted badly. I'll never forget that call in my life.

On the day of the appointment, we spent three minutes or less on small talk even though Arthur could have spent an hour catching up with his old friend. I almost fell off of my chair when Arthur asked, "Would you give my friend Steve some business?" - Now his friend had two options, either "yes" or "no." He said "yes"!

It might have taken me six months to get to that point with this very large company but Arthur knew he could be direct with his very good business friend. I use this story often when I'm in front of a group of salespeople because it illustrates the value of using contacts and referrals. Going over your contact list every three to six months and asking your customers, friends, and acquaintances for referrals should be on going. Use any "tool" in your toolbox to shorten that decision cycle. Offer your help on a regular basis to your contacts. Watch out for business opportunities for your clients. Give them referrals often…….you get what you give.

Help others with your contacts, **Ralph Waldo Emerson, in his "Essay on Compensation" said "the undisputable law of this Universe is that you get what you give." (there's that law again).** If you want people to give you referrals, give them. Your book antennae should always be up for opportunities to help others. Help your customers and prospects that you meet do more business, be ready to introduce others to them that will help them. Help other sales people that you know grow their business and they will want to help you.

Networking fits in with this strategy because it's giving to others. In networking, you shall reap as you sow. Cold calling is a waste of time in my opinion. The return for the time spent is often very low when you add in the burn out factor. Sale people, who rely solely on cold calling, burn out and turnover at a very high rate. We know this and yet most sales training is still focused on cold calling. If you are going to cold call, make it five a day on outrageously big targets. Set your sites on the biggest and best customers you can dream of and cold call them. Call the President. That way, the risk and reward ratio makes the effort worthwhile.

The same could apply to your networking. You could be working with the best and brightest in similar industries, helping them to get business. Sowing this you would reap, over time, a harvest of the best and brightest people helping you and introducing you to new prospects. The difference is that with Networking, you would be invited in perhaps even personally introduced at a lunch or dinner meeting. Even one warm call a week would beat the best week of cold calling. The key to effective networking is effective sowing. I hear people complain "I'm not getting anything from my group." What do you think they sowed in spring to reap a harvest of "not getting anything"? The rule does not apply sometimes; it applies every time. As Dr. Ivan Misner, founder of BNI (Business Networking International) says, "Givers Gain. That is the motto of BNI.

Start by selecting your sites to plant. Would you plant a garden in a field of rocks, thorns, trees and scrub bushes? Do some research, ask questions. Look for groups that fit your particular occupation or business. Once selected, attend a few meetings to be sure that they call on similar types of customers and do not compete with you. How do they present themselves? How do they dress? Do they behave professionally? Would you refer these people? What are they sowing in the world? If they are sloppy and careless with their dress and their words, what kind of clients and prospects do you think are part of their harvest? Take your time here and do the due diligence. When you have found the group that fits, plant the seed and join. Now begins the springtime of your membership. Things will look messy here. The beginning of your membership in any group will feel that way. Take time here to plant deeply and carefully. Meet each member out for breakfast or lunch. Find out how you can help them. Be prepared for the meeting. Show them how professional you are. Keep your word, do everything you say you will do even if it hurts. Do not break appointments, arrive late, or worse, arrive unprepared. Take notes in your meeting, note the personal facts. Birthdays, anniversaries, children's names, spouse name, quirky facts that you can acknowledge at a later date. Remember, you are sowing here. Also, be aware during the meeting if the person is interested in what you do. Are they asking how they could help you? Remember they will be showing you how they sow a crop as well. If they do not reflect the kind of crop that you want to plant, offer to help them with some ideas that you have about growing their business or better, give them this book. If they still do not fit, tell them why and if they are open to help, give it. If not, move on to preserve your future harvest. If you feel good about working with the person, work on getting them a referral or introduction. Offer to link their website to yours. Feature them or their business in your newsletter. Send a personal letter introducing them to your top 10 customers. As you work to help them plant so will you reap the same. Be patient. No rushing to the harvest.

Instead of joining a group to network in, you could do the same with a few respected business people who you know or would like to know, that call on the same types of customers as you and you do not compete with them. You could call them and say that you respect them and have heard great things about them and that you call on similar types of customers. Note that you do not compete and that you were thinking that you could help them grow their business. Suggest that you meet for lunch. Start the same process as above. The goal would be to find four or five people that you could work with to develop what BNI calls a contact sphere.

**TIP: "Warm calls are better than cold calls"*

The key to prospecting is setting a goal of "warming up" the calls. Offer seminars that educate your prospect, do not sell at these events. Warm calls require that you get to know your prospect and they get to know you. Whatever your industry, offer an informative seminar educating on an important aspect of what you do. Give real information. What you give you get. When you give real information, your prospects will learn something and appreciate that you did not attempt to sell them. At the beginning of the seminar ask the attendees to take out a business card and turn it over. Ask them to put the letters Y N TIO on the card. At the end of the seminar tell them what the letters stand for. Y=yes, N= no, TIO= think it over. You tell them to cross out think it over unless they are willing to accept a call from you within 48 hours and tell you "yes" or "no." Under those circumstances it would be ok to circle TIO. If not, then they must circle Yes or No. Tell the no's you will call to ask what they liked about the seminar and to ask what could have been improved. Tell them that they can circle yes if they would like to hear more about what you taught them. Tell them that you will call to set an appointment.

Design a post card that you can mail to target prospects. Most people at least look at a postcard to decide whether to throw it out or not. Mail it to the top 15 or 20 prospects on your list each week for four weeks and then call. You can ask if they have gotten your post card. You can ask if they remember throwing out the one that looked like yours. Again, the goal is to warm up the call.

Go over your customer list and ask for referrals. Do this every six months or so. Ask your top customers how you can help them get business. What is it that they are looking for? You cannot do this for everyone, although your top customers would appreciate a referral too. And remember you get what you give.

Think of ways to warm up the call first, then call.

*TIP: Make your daily goal to meet new people and HAVE FUN.

By making your daily goal, meeting say five new people that you can discover whether or not they ever buy what you sell, you take the pressure off of yourself to sell something right away. You are new at selling so, the more people you meet and ask "how can you help them?", you begin building a network of new contacts that will get to know you. You can think of it as "I am having fun meeting people that I can help and will help me someday." You can ask the new people you meet things like "what do they look for in an ideal customer?" Ask them about their business, how have they been doing it, how did they get started, how did they get their current position, etc..... get to know them, remember your developing a relationship, not making a sale.... yet.

What better way to operate then to make it your goal to meet new people? You do not suffer any rejection.

Ask them for help. You could say "I am just starting out and I am looking for advice on how to grow my business, who would you call on if you were me?"

Most important of all, have FUN! Look forward to who you will meet each day and with wonder about who you might meet. Keep a smile on your face and let the world know you are having fun. See what that kind of enthusiasm will bring you.

TIP: "When you cold call, make them BIG, real BIG."

Cold call five top prospects each day. Since cold calling is has the lowest odds of success make your targets "**_outrageous*_**." Cold call accounts that you only dream about.... Remember, your dreams can come true, why not start here?

Call at the top (who calls the president anyway?). Cold call only the top prospects in your targeted market. Since the odds aren't great go for it. With 25 calls per week on top prospects even with a 2% return on 1250 calls annually that would give you 25 appointments with the top prospects in your market.

Russell Conwell used to say, "There are diamonds in your backyard." Your diamond mine is your customer list. Mine it weekly or monthly depending on how large the list is. Ask your customers "who do they know who might introduce you to a company you want to do business with or who could they recommend you to. These diamonds are sitting on the ground, compared to cold calling. With cold calling, you have to dig the mine first. Referrals from your existing customers are like diamonds in a stream. If you have dealt with everyone with integrity and given to each what you want to get, if you have left everyone a little better than you found them in every moment, your customers will gladly help. You will get what you have been giving.

14. Develop new behaviours/ Love being better than you were yesterday

Don't wait for management to review you - Ask what I did today to:

- Get closer to my goals?
- Get closer to my income needs?
- Train my customers?

- Get more productivity and customers?

Great sales people review themselves constantly! I used to wonder why salespeople who worked for me, waited for me to review them, and quite frankly, I wondered why I needed them.

One of the reasons that someone might want to review themselves daily would be the goal of "Personal Improvement." We all have personal habits that are holding our sales back **Jim Rohn, the powerful motivational speaker and the nation's premier business philosopher has said "the harder he works on himself, the better his business does."** Ask your boss for the things he or she would like to see you improve. Ask your family and friends as well. Most of the things you will hear, you already knew deep down inside, but until you take inventory, you won't improve. Then prioritize that list starting with number one. Ask your prospects what went wrong after a lost sale, or what they liked about your competitor's offering?

Once you've set your sights on your personal improvement, be patient with yourself. Work on one at a time. Visualize yourself doing the new behaviour you're looking for.

I can't count the number of times I've heard a salesperson or even sales managers categorize they or their employees as one type of sales person or another. Does this sound familiar? He or she is not a

- Detail orientated person.
- Organized person.
- Closer
- Opener
- Maintainer

Aren't these the actual things that are holding you back? Be honest. Never accept these things as the "Proverbial You." Remember, you become what you thing about. Change them. You can. Think instead "What do you want to become and starting with the end in mind, think about what new behaviours would be required to become that type of person and begin to act like you are that person now. Those new behaviours would become your new habits in as soon as 21 days. Do it.

TIP: You are what you say you are

TIP: "Love Being Better"

Say this to yourself daily. Tell your boss that you love being better. Make it your focus and the little things will become easier, instead of being **tremendous** annoyances.

People love doing business with people who are good at what they do. So, make it your goal to be better every day. Your customers, boss, and co-workers will notice and respect you.

All those around you will want to do what they can to help you. They will want to do it well because they know that you do things well.

If you are **sloppy** don't be surprised if your support team is sloppy. If customers recognize that you are haphazard don't be surprised if they take advantage of this.

But if you work at being the best everyday (try it) you'll be amazed at how this effects, in a wonderful positive way, those around you. Try it at home as well. Your family will react positively towards you as well. By loving being better, you'll find each day will be more fun.

Work with passion. All too often we choose jobs that we do not love - that do not fill us with passion. We take our lunch pail and work like "serfs in the kingdom" for our masters.

Love what you do -jobs without passion dry the blood in our veins, make our bones brittle and worse - break our souls. If selling is what you can do with a passion, then do it. If not, find the passion. Eleanor Roosevelt once said, "You must do the one thing that you think you cannot do!" Think about how that might change your life. Just Do It.

My goal each day is to "leave everyone and everything a little better than I find them." This helps me be fully present in each moment. I do not have to worry about the future or regret the past if I am fully focused on the present. This is the only moment that we ever have. If I am fully present in every moment the future takes care of itself. I have my goals and dreams and I am only focused on the moment that I have before me.

TIP: This is the only moment we ever have.

When you are always doing your best, you are in "use", honouring your Source, God, the Divine or whatever your Higher Power is for you. You are building your Universal resume. Giving your best means you will get the best in return.

TIP: "Manage your life, not the lives of others"

A busy body in sales should be just that, busy with their business and not that of others. I call it the "general manager of the universe syndrome. Mind your own business. Stay out of the office gossip and politics. I once worked with group of people who spent more time doing other people's jobs and engaging in office politics. This was a terrible waste of energy and their sales showed it.

Of course, by talking about everyone else, they were deflecting blame from themselves, but the truth was that the result each of these people was getting was lack lustre. Let me share with you a quote from Gandhi:

"A true soldier does not argue as he marches, how success is going to be ultimately achieved. But he is confident that if only he plays his humble part well, somehow or other the battle will be won. It is in that spirit that every one of us to know how to do our own part well!"

Make written comments and suggestions every quarter to your management. This is a professional's method of contributing. Stay out of office politics.

Imagine the energy it takes to manage all the affairs of those around you. Some people are "drama addicts." They spend a considerable amount of their time caught up in another person's drama. **Jeffrey Gittomer in his book "The Little Red Book of Selling says "the less time you spend in other people's business and other people's drama, the more time you'll have for your own success."**

I realized, about 10 years ago, or so, that I could have so much more time in my life if I spent more time managing my life and less managing the lives of those around me. People and events were things that I could not control anyway, so why waste the time and energy? I decided to give it up.

From that moment on, I spent most of my energy managing me. Now, mind you, I say most of my energy. I am human and I do catch myself in the drama of others from time to time. I notice it faster and as soon as I do, I get back on track. Many people around me note that I accomplish much and have a lot on my plate. It's not difficult for me to manage more because I am only managing my stuff most of the time. Those same people complain that they do not have enough time. If they gave up their role as "general manager of the universe" they would add enormous amounts of time and energy to their day. What they accomplish in life would increase dramatically. The minute you go in a new direction, make a new choice, new results appear. It's a law of the Universe. The Universal Law of Cause and Effect. More on that law later.

15. Remember that "What goes around, comes around"

Look in the mirror wherever you are in your sales career, you are responsible for it. You are just where you should be according to your thoughts and actions. Accept it. Don't beat yourself up over it, but face it. Others are not to blame; the company is not to blame, nor your co-workers, and not your parents - **YOU ARE.** Remember this: "Incompetents invariably make trouble for people other than themselves!" © by Larry McMurtry

Whenever I work with people who are blaming everyone in their company for their lack of performance, I like to hand them a mirror. People who are always blaming others for their lack of success are only deflecting the blame from themselves. So, accept it-it's yours - then move on. You are the creator of your life. Warner Erhard once said "I accuse you of being a circumstance in your life." If you are a circumstance, then you are in "victim" mode. If you believe that things are happening to you, then you are in victim mode. Things have not happened to you; you have created these events. You are attracting the events and people that you need to see in order to grow. That's why it happens that certain events or people continually show up in our lives.

**TIP: You are the creator of your life.*

Until we see it and learn a new behaviour, we are destined to repeat the events or meet similar types of people. You cannot grow until you accept the responsibility, but don't linger over it. Instead, learn from your past, in fact laugh. Yes, laugh at your past (you're not the only one with a past) then write down some goals for personal improvement. Do you think that professional athletes linger long over the missed putt, the crash on the first turn, the strike out, the fumble, the wild pitch? The successful one's certainly do not. Just keep your eyes on where you intend to be, not on where you have been. Use the past as a lesson or sign posts, so that you do not take that same road over and over. Here is a poem that I wrote over ten years ago, for people who worked for me (at least that is what I thought, back when I wrote it). I came to realize a few years later that I wrote it for me. I was the biggest obstacle in my life and I had my head in a bad place as you will see.

IT CAN'T BE ME

By Stephen P. Lentini

Lots of people do better than me

I bitch and moan, kick and scream,
I am unable to reach my dream.

I work hard, I think I'm smart

It's those around me, it's their part.
They're the reason, I've failed to start.

They keep me down I know it's true
At every turn, it's me they screw.

And so, it goes, every day.
I get Up and I'm on my way.

Convinced I'm not to blame -it can't be me,
what a shame!

Wait, was that a mirror I just passed, no way, can't be,
that person had their head up they're a_ _!

*TIP: "Remember, you reap what you sow.
What goes around comes around"*

"Respect nature and learn from the seasons"

What is the result now of your last springtime? Are you reaping a bountiful harvest? What you are currently harvesting in the direct result of the quality and amount of "seeding" that you did last spring. Did you select the proper soil? Did you neglect to inspect the seeds? Did you take proper care to prepare the ground before planting? Nature provides us with a perfect model to follow and yet we humans think that these same patterns do not apply to our lives. We expect to reap a bountiful harvest even though we rested or procrastinated when we should have been planting. Think about the kind of harvest you want before you plant. Sow lies, reap lies. Sow lack of integrity, reap a lack of integrity in return. Sow procrastination, reap a bleak future. Sow honesty, reap honesty. Sow loyalty and commitment, reap loyalty and commitment in return. The one thing that we forget is that nature returns more than what is sowed by many thousands of times over. Just think, from that one tomato seed you sow, the tomato plant returns thousands of seeds. The same is true in our lives. The Law is the Law. **Jim Rohn says in his book "The Seasons of Life", "Faith further provides to us an irrevocable law decreed in heaven which assures that for every disciplined human effort we will receive a multiple reward...for each cup planted, a bushel reaped.** Whatever we choose to put into the soil of life will surely return to us multiplied. That is why if we sow inaction, we reap a future of despair. What are you sowing in your business or on the job? What about at home and with your family and friends? Can you honestly say that you sow love, forgiveness, gratitude and understanding? What would the harvest be from seeds such as these especially with the guarantee of a multiplied return?

What you expect to harvest begins with the seeds and the discipline of preparing and planting in the spring. It's never too late to begin you planting anew. Start now. After planting your seeds of your new future, resist the urge to "rush to the harvest." Humans always want to rush to harvest in their lives. Would you plant an apple tree seed and then stand over it saying "ok, where are the apples? No, of course we wouldn't. It sounds ridiculous, and yet that is exactly what we do in lives. Very often, we expect quick results or riches. We want to "rush to the harvest." Instead, during your winter of planning for your next harvest, write down, in addition to what seeds you will plant, a plan for nurturing the crop. Allow enough time for your seeds to sprout, grow and develop a young crop and then a bountiful harvest is more likely. Allow time for the full cycle of seasons, one cannot rush nature and that is her message for us as well. Also, allow for bugs and pests, (negative events and people), an early frost or any bad weather. In this way, you will not be deterred from your plan of a bountiful harvest. Spring is a time for persistence and perseverance. In my sales training and seminars over the last 7 years I have often asked my clients, "what would spring look like if the daffodils, crocus and tulips said "oh, there's too many rocks in the way, the ground is too hard, or it's too cold, I think I'll quit." Do not quit when it looks like things are difficult.

***TIP: The Universe tests everything purposefully, to eliminate those that would give in. To weed out the one's that do not belong.
You will be tested. The tests, firm our resolve, if we do not give in.***

There are tools required to prepare the ground and to plant properly. Just as the farmer requires the proper tools and equipment to prepare and plant, so to it is with us. The tools required for a good planting are a positive attitude, giving what we want to get, action, forgiveness, patience, love, gratitude, opening up, measuring and tracking, visualization, acting as if, speaking as if, change and awareness of choice. All of these things together will bring us a new harvest, one unlike the past. Without choice and change, we would use all of the other tools to sow but we would reap the same past harvest over and over. We must be willing to expand and go beyond where we have sown before with all of the above. For each of the tools mentioned are separate crops as well. Depending on how you use them, you are sowing a future harvest from each of them. Whatever we sow in forgiveness for example we reap when we require forgiveness ourselves. Whatever we have sown in love, patience or action, we too have reaped. If we work continually to expand where we have gone before, like the Universe is expanding, we will reap a harvest of many new benefits. Jim Rohn says in his book "The Seasons of Life", "The act of planting during the warm breezes of spring requires that we exert the pain of human discipline and being unwilling to do so assures that in the coming fall, we shall surely experience the greater pain of regret – the difference is that the pain of discipline weighs ounces, and the pain of regret weighs tons. We must either plant during the springtime of our life, or beg from others during the fall."

TIP: "GIVE what you want to get" (are you getting the message?)

Prosperity is related to what you are thinking about in every moment.

***TIP: If you are always worried that
there isn't enough, there won't be.***

Your outer world reflects your inner world. Remember what Earl Nightingale said, "You become what you think about." If your predominant thought pattern is about being frustrated, your outer world will reflect frustration back to you. If there never seems to be enough money look at what you were taught at home about money. Was lack the predominant pattern at home. "Money doesn't grow on trees." Remember that one? Look also at your giving. You need to look at every level of giving. Are you generous? Would your family or friends describe you as giving? Are you generous with your money, time, forgiveness, love, consideration, etc.? Get into action giving more of everything that you have and give what you want to get. Look at all the areas above, love, time, forgiveness, consideration, appreciation, praise, acknowledgement, etc. Would you like to have more of all of those things? Get into action giving what you want to get.

One of the Universal Laws is "You can't give what you don't have." Research Tithing. All of the most successful people tithe! John D. Rockefeller's first tithe was $9.00. He ended his life having tithed over $500 million dollars. And don't forget, he started in the 1800's and died in the early 1900's. What would that be worth in today's dollars? When asked about his wealth he would say, "GOD gave me my money. If you begin tithing even if you think you do not have the funds to do it, the universe will support your decision because you must have it to give it. You are "acting as if." Start with giving 10% of what you have left after paying everything including yourself. The theory of tithing is that you are honouring a higher power. Tithing says that you have faith that you will be taken care of. After all, even the smallest creatures on earth are taken care of, why not you? Money will begin to appear for you. I started tithing 10% of my net pay over 20 years ago. During my health challenge, I was out of work for six months. I had over $24,000 come in the mail to me from people who had heard of my circumstances in just over 3 months. I did not need disability insurance (and I did not have any). Today I tithe 10% of my gross pay and 20% of my training, speaking events and 30% of my book sales. Each year I add more and more income and I give out more and more. There is always plenty to spare and share. I figure that I did not come here with any money and that I will not leave with any, so that I must be here to manage it and have fun with it and I do. Give what you want to get.

16. Motivate, Motivate, Motivate

*TIP: "Motivate yourself and lead by example to
motivate those around you"*

Read everything pertaining to sales and to personal growth as a way to keep your motivation high. Read about how the Universe works and how successful people have a Higher Power in their life. Read "Think and Grow Rich, and the Universal Laws of Success" by Napoleon Hill. Read "As a Man Thinketh" by James Allen. Read books by Wayne Dyer, Deepak Chopra, Mark Victor Hansen, Jack Canfield and Jim Rohn. Read books on selling like "The Sales Bible and the Little Red Book of Selling" by Jeffrey Gittomer. Read "Selling is Dead" by Marc T. Miller and Jason M. Sinkovitz.

And read "The Power of a Positive No" by William Ury and "The World's Greatest Salesman" by Og Mandino.

Develop your relationship with your Higher Power, as you define it. God, The Universe, The Divine, however you see the energy all around us, as a way to understand why you are here and motivating yourself will be easy. You can leave all the hard stuff to your higher power and do what is on your plate to do in each moment and leave the rest up to her or Him.

Read biographies about successful people or about anyone you admire.

Absorb them and consider adding to your own personality, a trait or strategy you found interesting. If it worked for others why not give it a try. If you will not read, isn't that the same as someone who cannot read? Isn't the long-term effect the same? Books on tape, or CD or on an iPod or MP3 are the same thing. Just find a way to do it.

Buy the books, buy the one day or two day seminars to get incremental changes in your behaviour. Invest in reinforcement training that pertains to behavioural and attitude training- not techniques only. This type of training is usually conducted over a long period of time. They vary from 12 weeks to three years or more. If you own or owned a company, or are employed as a salesperson, you are challenged today to motivate your sales support team to help you reach your goals. Teach, train, build, and respect our support staff. Listen to them. Push the cart, don't whip the ox. Help them; help you get where you want to go. Include them, perhaps in the success. I've heard many salespeople say, "it's their job, they get paid to support me and it's what I expect." True, but do you think their support team went the extra mile for them. No way. Find a way to make it fun. Find a way for your team to get a win. Everyone loves winning. Sports Teams know the objective with each game and they know who won in the end. Come up with something your support team can win daily, weekly, or monthly. Give them a reason to cheer and celebrate the win if they achieve it.

Have integrity. Do what you say. Your employees are watching and will know in an instant if you say one thing and do another.

Don't forget the losses. But review them in a blame proof atmosphere and to remind your team - they take the field again tomorrow. A win is only around the corner. Put together a crew of committed others to support you.

Acknowledge and praise them. Send them notes of appreciation and thanks. Ask them what they would like in a gift and send them the gift, whatever it takes to let them know that you care. If people know you care you can demand more.

17. Dream and believe in Possibilities

That's right. Dream, daydream, picture yourself where it is you want to be. Dream it. Believe it. Do it. Use your imagination machine. Your imagination power and manifest your deepest desires.

***TIP: Whatever it is you hope to achieve - Dream it.**

Visualize the goal and the rewards of achieving it. Spend some time alone -at the beach, in the woods, wherever you find peace, - and see yourself doing what you want. Imagine yourself with the rewards of dream - the big boat, the fame, the power, the money, whatever you want - be there, at your goal, in your dreams. Imagine yourself with the family love and support, imagine yourself satisfied with what you have, Be grateful. Feel what it feels like to be always grateful. The most successful people in sports visualize the outcome they want.

Do it. Selling will become easier when you see your outcomes first.

To assist your visualizing process, spend some quiet time each day if you can or at least weekly. Create an image book that has pictures, Quotes, affirmations, incantations and words that support your goals. Look at it twice daily, once when you first get up and before you go to sleep. Studies have shown these times to be the most powerful times to impress anything on your subconscious mind. **Begin to "act as if"** you were already what you wanted to become and act like you already have what you wanted to have.

If satisfaction and fulfilment in life is your number one goal, begin to act as if you were satisfied and fulfilled already. My teacher, Toni Stone says that "satisfaction is first a decision, feelings follow." She teaches that if one is not satisfied now, then they will never be satisfied later. They will always be satisfied…. when? When this happens or that happens, that is when they will be satisfied. The key is to be satisfied now, so that you will always be in a satisfied state of mind. There is no in between, if you are not satisfied, you will never be satisfied. Make the decision now, be satisfied.

Intention and visualization work together to help us manifest our deepest desires. Get the book, The Power of Intention by Wayne Dyer. Use visualization along with intending what you desire daily. Rent the movie "What the Bleep Do We Know and The Secret." Study the Law of Attraction. Your thoughts, words and actions have power. Einstein said that "there is no power greater than the power of imagination." Imagine yourself succeeding, dream dreams beyond where your mortal mind tells you what is possible. Have that "BHAG" goal, as Mark Victor Hansen recommends, that Big Hairy Audacious Goal. Why not? You can imagine anything. Feel what it would feel like to arrive at your goal. See the celebration. All of these steps contribute towards you reaching your goal.

Visualization has great power to bring one quicker to where one wants to go.

Dream On
By Stephen P. Lentini

Dream on, don't quit,
Dreamers seem to never fit.

They're off to lands,
We know not where,

But then again, we'll never dare.
Believe you must! Is what they say,
Soon will come a golden day.
Never ever lose sight of it.
Please. Please. Don't ever quit.

Keep on dreamin',
it's what you must,
if you'll ever see what you think just

"I have no patience with people who are always raising difficulties."
- ***Winston Churchill***

Possibilities, on the other hand are another story. I cannot say for sure although it's a safe bet that Churchill preferred people who believed in possibilities.
****TIP: Even during your most difficult times look
for possibilities and opportunities.***

Each occurrence in our life holds a new opportunity, whether it is for personal or monetary growth. By always looking for the possibilities for growth, growth will come. Believe it.

Your imagination knows no limits. Imagine your future. Napoleon Hill and Ernest Holmes once said that "you would not have the desire for something if you did not have the ability to bring it forth." If you feel a desire to achieve something special in your life…. imagine it and feel what it feels like to have already achieved it….and then get on to doing it.

18. Integrity, keep your Word and do what you said

How can you expect your clients to be impeccable with their word if you are not impeccable with your own? As a professional sales person, you are responsible for helping your prospects be impeccable with their word. When you hear a prospect use words that sound wishy-washy, it is your job to call them on it. What I use as my guide is "no lie goes by me un-addressed." How about your company or with your boss? Are you willing to be the stand for integrity with your company or your boss?

For example, if a client or prospect says "you are looking good on this project", "you are real close", you might say "I appreciate the fact that we are close", "occasionally when I have heard we are close in the past it has turned out to mean that we were not getting the order", "that is probably not the case here is it?"

How can you call people on their wishy-washy words if you use them yourself? Listen to the words others around you use for the next two weeks. See if you can spot the times where you could ask, "What do you mean when you say ……."

Better yet, listen to your own words. Are you wishy-washy with those around you? Are you often less than direct with people to soften the effect of what you are saying? Do you make promises you have no intention of keeping? If you are not impeccable with your own words you will never hold those around you accountable for what they say, least of all a prospect.

Do you have integrity?

Can you be counted on to keep your word? Ask others how you show up, how do they view you when it comes to keeping your word. Ask them to rate you on a scale of 1 – 10. Ask your spouse or significant other. Ask your Boss.

Clean up any lack of integrity that you find in yourself. Remember that you reap what you sow, what are you sowing with your word?

I worked at a company where an issue came up with a former client. The client had just left the company where he was a member. It was a group organization. I had promised him that he qualified for our special program that would pay him an extra 1% of the monies that he had received over the previous twelve months. It would mean $13,000+ to his company. I checked with my boss at the time of the special request and she too gave her word that he did in fact qualify for our special program. When he left our group, my boss and the President of the company did not want to pay him…because he had lied about whether he was staying with us as a member of the group. Regardless, we gave our word and I told my boss and the President that "it did not work for me that we were not going to keep our word" and that my request was that we pay him. It took six weeks of discussion, and eventually my boss and the President of the company agreed that it was more important to keep our word with this guy even though he lied. I understood the emotions and all the feelings about being lied to by this member and still, we gave our word. Our integrity and my own integrity were worth more than the $13,000+....it was priceless. Be a stand for integrity, even if you lose your job over it, would you want to be working for a company that breaks it word and is willing to put a price on its integrity?

TIP: Don't' sell it if you wouldn't buy it.

Don't' sell more than someone needs to fill your bank account. Help your prospects buy, listen to what their needs are and make sure that they are a good fit for your company or that what you sell is a good solution for them. If you have integrity, you will be sure to recommend that they buy something else or from someone else if they are not a fit. You have integrity if that is what you do. If you sell only to take care of your bank account, you will always be working hard to fill it. If you oversell someone, eventually they discover it. How do you think they feel about you? How do they feel about your company? What do you think that they will tell others about you?

Your lack of integrity will catch up with you, what goes around comes around, remember the law of cause and effect. Have integrity, if you take good care of others with integrity, they will take care of your bank account gladly. They will tell others and your circle of cash will grow by referral. You will not have to worry about the future if you take great care of the present moment. If you are experiencing difficulties now, it is because of your lack of integrity during sometime past. Forget it and start cleaning it up now. Start doing the right thing now. Have integrity and the Universe and your customers will reward that effort.

19. Stop the Whining and Start the Winning

I've met and worked with salespeople who whined more than a six-year-old who wanted that new toy. The time that they spent whining could have been spent calling a new prospect for an appointment. I had no patience for these people because their whining sapped my energy. Stay away from whiners - they sap your energy. If you are a whiner, stop. Use the energy for winning. Think of all that time you have spent whining as wasted. You could have been selling. As soon as you catch yourself whining, stop it. Gradually this stupid habit will disappear and you will see that you have more time for selling and winning.

TIP: Your world is formed from the inside out.

Your world is an out picturing of your predominant thought patterns. Negative thinking creates a negative experience. If you don't like your experience of the world, change how the world is experiencing you.

You are the only one in this life that you can control. As you change, things will change. Track your responses to the people and events in your life. Where are, you reacting the same way over and over and expecting a different outcome. Step back from those people, prospects, bosses, family, etc. and think about what would be a new response for you? What would be something new to say or do? When you do, you will start to see a new life form right before your eyes and the only one who changed was you.

TIP: Want a positive experience? Think positive thoughts.

Good selling requires a lot of energy. Great selling requires even more. So, guard your energy levels by staying positive, and keeping away from negative people. This includes customers, co-workers, bosses, and spouses –whomever.

If you are working in a negative company, get out. Move on - there's a big world out there and a life beyond the company you are at. If the company cannot support your efforts, first find a way to support your company. Suggest new ways of doing things. Complain with a request or suggestion. If this does not work, find a new company.

If you are working in a negative company, get out. Move on - there's a big world out there and a life beyond the company you are at. If the company cannot support your efforts, first find a way to support your company. Suggest new ways of doing things. Complain with a request or suggestion. If this does not work, find a new company.

Usually negative people are unable to change. This is who they are and how they view the world.

Surround yourself with people who see possibilities and let no one put obstacles up between you and your goals. Once you have your goals set, guard your energy. Say it out loud. Practice saying "Sorry – believing it cannot happen or that we are blocked in any way from succeeding does not work for me." "Can we focus on what would work or how to get around this temporary obstacle?"

*TIP: Remind yourself frequently
"Your energy is one of your most important assets."*

You will find yourself identifying time and energy draining people and customers, and successfully avoiding them. Selling will be a lot easier and more fun.

I know it's the old cliché but - refuse to let negative thoughts into your mind. Try picturing a door in your mind and when a negative thought enters close the door, say "thank you for sharing and close the door.

Use affirmations! Anything that follows the words "I am" is an affirmation. You are the programmer of your mind. Listen to the words you are currently using in your everyday conversations. You will be amazed to hear some of the things that you are programming. Be clear, direct and concise in your words and amazing things will follow.
*TIP: "Speak about what's intended, that's a way to win"

Think about all the negative events in your life? Did you think about them casually before they happened? Did you ever casually wish for something that appeared later in your life?

When you can see that you have created all the negative events in your life you will see your own power to create. You will see just how powerful you are. Get on purpose with your thoughts and words. Have them match what you long for. Whatever is your deepest longing, go for it. Eleanor Roosevelt once said, "You must do what you think you cannot do!" Get on purpose with your thinking and speaking. Remember, you have created your world up until now without disciplined thinking or a focused effort.

*TIP: Just think what a powerful future you could create
if you disciplined your thoughts and focused your efforts totally
on your deepest desires.*

Listen carefully to what you speak about, journal your thoughts for a week, month, a quarter or a year or more. You will see that you are the creator of your circumstances. You are not at the effect of your circumstances. You are a powerful co –creator of your world. I say co-creator because I believe in a higher power in my life. I think about the fact that we live in a galaxy, in a Universe often. I believe that I can tap into that power to create what I deeply desire. You can too. I have a coach and the support of others to help me stay on track. Disciplined and focused. I am achieving my deepest desires, you can too.

19. Be Grateful

It is not enough to think to yourself "well I am grateful" once in a while.

TIP: Gratitude is something that is practiced like exercise.

To really see results in your life you must be in gratitude for everything. Because I have been studying gratitude for many years and been speaking and writing what I was grateful for, I have prospered in ways unimaginable to me before I started the practice. By speaking of gratitude and developing an awareness of being in a state of gratitude, I learned just how resentful and bitter I was without realizing it. When I started by actually saying out loud what I was grateful for, my brain would respond with "you're not grateful, who are you kidding? I was surprised to learn just how ungrateful I really was.

As I said earlier, one afternoon, I was training a group of sales people, one second I was fine and the next I needed an ambulance. While I was being attended to, by the EMT's, I was saying how grateful I was for the experience. I know they must have thought that I was crazy, but I knew that great things were coming to me at that moment. I knew that this health challenge was the flood, the forest fire in my life. I had asked God "to clear the path" for me, so that I would clearly see what was mine to do in this world. Within a month or so, the health challenge appeared. Little did I know then that it was to be a six-month ordeal. I was in the hospital for sixty days straight, and over half of the next two months for a total of 100 days... It would take almost a year before I would return to normal. Even on the way to Intensive Care, I was grateful. My whole life has changed since and gratitude is the key. The whole time seemed like just a few days. And yes, I had a few blue moments and there were tears, but they only lasted hours, sometimes just minutes. Imagine, I could have been bitter for the whole experience.

*TIP: Practice Gratitude. Say what you are grateful for
and write what you are grateful for every day.*

You will become grateful even for what you currently define as awful, because you will see the gift later because of gratitude. Try it and see. Call or write me with your experiences.

21. We do live in a Galaxy, in a Universe

Take some quiet time each day, preferably 6am and 6pm to reflect on the fact that we live in a Galaxy, in a Universe. During my health challenge, I had a moment in intensive care that truly changed the rest of my life. I was in the hospital for a little over four days, since Wednesday, now Monday afternoon and my friend Warren and my significant other, Janice, (now my soon to be wife), were visiting me. I remember seeing Janice and Warren one second, being in the hospital room with them and the next second I was in another room, large room. There were a lot of people in the room. I remember hearing and seeing someone speaking at the front of the room. I remember thinking, "Oh someone is speaking, I better move closer to hear what they are saying." I moved closer and realized that it was someone that I worked with that was speaking, a voice was giving a eulogy and this person had touched a lot of lives. It was as if I was seeing my future. I remember thinking, "oh, this person has touched a lot of lives, I wonder who it is. I better move closer to hear who it is." In the next second I realized that it was my own eulogy. Next I was asked, very gently, very lovingly, "Stay or go." That was it, nothing else. I remember in that moment feeling very peaceful and thinking "well, I have touched a lot of lives, thy will be done." I surrendered my life to the will of the Universe, God or the Divine Consciousness. In that next second I was back in the hospital room. When I was comfortable with sharing that story some weeks later with Warren and Janice, Warren mentioned that "it must have been Monday, the doctor had asked us to contact your family as it did not look good….

I am certain that one of the reasons that I came back is to share this story that we are always safe, connected to the Divine, the Universe, living a miracle as well as living in a miracle in every moment. And that we have nothing to fear. To encourage people to live from the level of their soul and not the material world.

I have since remembered, not perfectly mind you, to surrender when I think that things are out of control. That I have nothing to fear since I have faced death and that even in death we have nothing to fear. We are safe always and in every moment. At the moment of my death there was no mention of anything I had achieved or failed to achieve. There was no mention of anything that I had acquired, nothing material at all. The only mention was of the people I had touched.

TIP: We have nothing to fear in this life.

How many of us live working hard to achieve and never stop to really be with and touch the people in our lives? How many of us really care, in each moment, of the other person in front of us? How many of us are only thinking of a quota or a promotion or the praise and accolades we will receive if we can "just close this customer?" Joseph Campbell has said "follow your bliss" and "The cave you fear to enter holds the treasure that you seek" Follow you bliss is to follow your heart's desire. Desire translated in Latin, is "of the Father" or "of the Universe."

TIP: Joseph Campbell said "you must let go of the life you have planned as to have the life that is waiting.

TIP: e.e. cummings once said 'to finally feel freedom, relax your grip and dive into the space."

Honour your desire and do what it takes to follow your dream. Even if it's part time while you work to pay the bills…remember to be present with everything and everyone as if it were your last day and as if you were living your dream life now. Remember my advice earlier to "act as if?" Act as if the desires of your heart were here already. God, the Divine the Goddess, the Universe is in the NOW. Be fully present in every moment always doing your best and your desires will manifest. Take the time to really be with your customers and prospects. Really feel what you are feeling and work to help your customers and prospects find the best solution for them even if it is not you. You get what you give and the Universe will reward you.

When you look up in the sky at night, we too are just one of those little twinkling stars. Physicists and astronomers, with the help of the Hubble telescope confirm now that just in our galaxy alone there are 200 billion + suns with planets that circle them. In our galaxy alone! We live in a miracle. Take time each day to reflect on that and remember to bring miracle thinking with you in each moment. The Universe is infinite, so bring some infinite possibility thinking with you as well. Imagine the energy that someone who thinks this way brings to every moment.

TIP: Thoughts have energy, so think about what you are sending to others with your thinking and think about bringing a miracle with you.

I salute the Diving in each person, silently and send them my blessings as a gift. This helps me to detach from the outcome and to remember that I do live in a Galaxy, in a Universe.

Don't worry about your quotas. Keep making sales calls, looking to help people buy and be fully present with them, intending to help them and you will be successful. I have been. Deepak Chopra, says in his book "Power, Freedom and Grace", "As you elevate your attention from the world of the humdrum and trivial to the world of the magical and miraculous, your life becomes magical and miraculous. Your attention is spontaneously alert to the fact that life itself is a miracle. And the more you put your attention on miracles, the more you become the conscious creator of miracles."

I urge you to bring your attention up to the level of the Divine, the miraculous in every moment. Even in those moments when someone or something is bothersome or difficult or even tragic. We cannot always see the miracle immediately or the reason for these difficult moments and usually sometime later we can see why they happened or how they contributed immensely to our growth, to our lives.

Try it for two or three years and see if you live a more joyful, successful, satisfied life.

22. Gaining and Keeping an Edge to Close More Sales, More Often

Gaining an edge means not looking like the sales teams or sales people of your competition. Most sales people do not study or grow after school whether it's college or high school. I have had business owners and sales people tell me "I haven't read anything since I got out of school." They know better than anyone how to do anything. They gain no edge. You can develop and edge by continually updating your "tool box" as I call it. Add to your repertoire by having a coach, reading/listening to everything you can about sales and leadership and personal growth.

Become the sales person who is so determined to have the "ideal clients" that you define and even help your company define who the ideal client is. Perhaps the top three ideal...a, b and c and then d is the walk away point. Characteristics of the ideal, second ideal and third ideal client from your own customer list as a company. The "walk away" point is easily defined to from those customers that take a lot of service time, are not productive, are always operating around the fringe of what is acceptable and knowing all the ideals and the "walk away", you can now develop questions to "help you and your future client hear whether you are a fit for them and you will hear if they are a fit for you.

You gain an Edge when you can help people buy because it is a different energy as opposed to selling. Selling is a pushing energy and you know people feel it...Haven't you? How did you feel when you are being pushed by a pushy salesy person? Helping someone buy is a "stepping back" energy, it's comfortable...it's perceptibly softer and yet it's still selling.

I suggest telling the future client exactly what your process is. "I am not here to sell you anything, I work to help you buy." "We work to help our clients buy the best solutions, even if it is not us." "I will have to ask what may seem like a lot of questions and my goal is to really understand what you are looking for, what your challenges are and what your thoughts are about what would work to solve the issue." "If at any point, you feel like we are not a fit, would you mind sharing that?" "That is my goal anyway so I don't mind hearing it if you feel it...ok?"

People ask me "Steve...how do I do that when my boss is asking me "what did you close lately..." I tell Leadership today they need to be asking "who have you met with...what did you talk about...who has problems we can solve and who did you walk away from and why?" If you are not walking away from clients that are not a fit, you are wasting time that could be spent with ideal future clients. Wouldn't you prefer your competition being bogged down by less than ideal clients anyway? Here is what you do to manage your boss...if they are not up to date on the cutting edge of managing sales teams...

Boss, here is the list of my behaviours this week...my meetings and notes of what we discussed...the characteristics of the top three ideal clients that I am looking for and a definition of clients that we don't want...and why...and how my meetings this week compared to this list. I have listed those too that I couldn't say yes to...and a few that turned around and those that are really a good ideal fit....

"What do you think boss?"

It doesn't matter what you sell, it can be software, medical devices, services and or B2B products or B2C products...today the energy that works best is "helping people buy" ...Why?

People have the internet and have done their shopping homework ahead of time and have defined in their mind what they want, now they are looking for either the best price (not on the ideal list typically on the "walk away") and or they are looking for the best people to buy from for service and to buy from people they like and most importantly trust.
I recently had five people call me out of the blue, one after five years another after three, two and etc..... asking me "Steve, what are you doing now...can you help me find new suppliers, new solutions, can you help me..., was the overriding theme..."

Why? After five and three years...amazing, right? Because they trust me implicitly ...I helped them back then buy the best solution and it turned out to be me and they know I had their best interest at heart...not mine ... I did not have "commission breath" as I call it.

Sales Veterans already have an edge called experience, passion for what they do and the ability to advise people based upon their experience. This is why former customers and clients call me. I have also learned from my teachers and coaches over the years how to manage and use the energy I project into the world. I teach sales people today to help customers and clients buy and that there is a subtle energy difference between selling and helping people buy. There also is the energy we can manage and in a cause and effect Universe it makes a huge difference in how hard we have to work and the resulting effect. I consciously project positive energy everywhere I go. I silently bless people, wish them happiness, joy and success and it makes a difference. Think of the energy you project like the wake a boat leaves behind. Everywhere you go, the energy you project onto the world creates a "wake of return to you and a wake of who you are." It tells everyone all about you without one word uttered. Tell your story to the Universe using positive energy and actions. Work to leave everyone and everything a little better than you find them in every moment. It makes a big difference. Think about the times people have said to you on the phone "are you ok" ....? Or think about the times you have asked others that question...the only thing on the phone you can sense is the energy they project ...you can't see them and yet you sense from the lower energy they are projecting that something is amiss. In person, it's times 10...body language and tonality make up 93% of the communication pie...words are only 7%...so if you feel a little blue or low ...fake it until you make it. Straighten up you posture and walk confidently...before your sales calls...use positive self-talk before your calls too. Use affirmative language such as "I am talented, I am valued and valuable, I am creative and energetic. I am enthusiastic and motivated. I am passionate and helpful. I bring positive results everywhere I go." ...etc.... Veterans can combine experience and the idea of managing the only thing you can effectively manage…. your SELF!!

Project consciously, positive energy by being a positive force…. everywhere you go all day long. Surround yourself with positive, strong, goal minded, prosperous people. Take an inventory of the people you surround yourself with from time to time and make sure you have slacked off. The sum total of the people you hang around with …whatever you would say about them are a reflection of your own mental state. Always do the right thing and the right things are returned to you. The Law of Cause and Effect is always working like gravity. WE can't see it…but rest assured it's working. If you are not getting back the results you want…change the cause…and that's you. I detach from outcomes in all situations in life and practice being fully present and mindful too…everywhere.

There are a few stories near the end of the book that really define detaching from outcomes and being mindful, fully present to help people.

Gaining an Edge means using all the skills you have learned about selling and subtly shifting your energy to understanding your future clients and clients' needs and being fully present to help them…they will feel this energy shift and trust your recommendations and let you challenge their thinking…even appreciate the challenge, welcome the challenge, if you are truly there for their best interest.

I teach this method and I have many testimonials from clients I have helped buy over the years and from my sales training clients now doing what I am teaching. It works amazingly well.

Herb Chambers Auto Dealerships, today owned by Warren Buffet Companies…have a few slogans I share often…

"You don't like car sales people and neither do we"
"We don't sell you a car…we help you buy one"

If this shift I am talking about has reached car dealers (not used folks yet I think) …helping people buy versus selling … don't you think it's time you gave yourself or you're team the same edge?

23. Business Strategy Coaching for the company and for the team.

What follows is a part of my business leadership coaching and strategy sessions outline.

Business Strategy Planning

Goal; Managing the behaviors of your team and enrolling them in the same;

   I.   Strategy –
   a.   Mid Vison (3years)

    b. Long Vision (5 and 10 years)
II. Define our culture
    a. Who are we and our "why"?
    b. Define mission
III. Ideal Clients
    I. Define Ideal clients using our existing customers, most profitable, most productive, respect us, pay us on time, etc.
    II. What is our "walk away" point?
    III. The process helps us develop questions for the sales team and support team to "help our customers buy" …whether it's us or not…we help future clients "hear" through the best questions, that we are a fit or not and we hear the same…we learn what we can say yes to and what we cannot say yes to.
    IV. Role of Leadership
        a) Boundaries – setting and managing, an ongoing journey, not a destination
        b) Helping department heads and sales team build the same process for their goals, within the company strategy that this process builds.
    V. Developing Limitless Possibility thinking
        a) How to develop and promote "limitless possibility" thinking
        b) Focus on solutions and not the problems once we understand the challenge before us

This process is about "managing your troop movements", Behaviors at all levels and enrolling teams and individuals in understanding and managing their behaviors daily and why it's helpful within a framework of the company's vision.
It's about building a plan of action that supports the company and it's about building a culture of personal growth, accountability and responsibility. Employees engaged in a culture of "helping each other win and the company win."

I help this process by facilitating it first with CEO's and then with Management and Department heads and with the Sales Team.

24. Managing the Culture for Growth* excerpt from "Lightning Growth"
by Justin Sachs and this chapter is by Steve Lentini pages 224-231

Having manged sales teams for the better part of 40 years and for the last 18 years trained, coached and consulted many companies in the area of sales what my experience has taught me about lightning growth is this; Managing the Culture is critical for growth and especially during challenges that any growing company will experience.

When the Biosphere 2 was built in Oracle Arizona, the idea was to demonstrate the viability of closed ecological systems to support and maintain human life in space colonization. (one intended use anyway).

When trees of many different shapes and sizes began to die, testing was done to discover why. Everything was tried…new food, fertilizer, water, more sun and less…nothing seemed to solve the problem. Trees would grow to certain height and then topple over. One windy day, a worker, as he came to work, and then entered the building…noticed what was missing…**the wind!** What they discovered as they varied the speed of the airflow into the building, the trees swaying back and forth, developed deeper, stronger roots. Small roots would break with the sway, and eventually new roots would develop off of the broken root and grow even deeper…much deeper.

It doesn't matter the industry or size of the company, the modern or mature…the challenges will come and the question is, **will your team withstand the hi winds?** It's your culture that will determine if your company will survive and it's your culture that will help provide lightning growth. Will you assist the company in developing deeper roots? Will you assist your employees in what's required to grow deeper? Do you want employees or a team of self-developed, enthused, positive, limitless thinkers?

What follows are my observations and stories from working with successful sales and company cultures and from working with cultures that were out of control. From what I have experienced, you can determine for yourself what direction to take…the question is this;

Will you do what it takes to manage your culture?

In 1982, I sold my distribution company to a large family owned company. Initially it was a big shock to my system. The culture was all about sales. Support departments were the brunt of criticism mostly, when things went wrong. Sales typically did not take any responsibility in helping the company perform productively. The company leadership as well had a responsibility as it seemed like the family did not know what to do, how to even address managing the culture. I'm not sure they even knew how out of control it was.

If something was out of stock, it was purchasing's problem. Instead of the sales team helping purchasing perform better and win, with usage projections when new customers were added, or when an existing customer began to purchases new items the company stocked, purchasing was beat up.

The same was true for warehouse and customer service. If mistakes were made…the out of control sales culture made the team around them wrong.

In my 16 years with the company, growth was emphasized over anything else and the culture suffered. There was never, not once, any training about how to support one another in winning. We all had the same goal and yet it seemed like we operated in different worlds. Never was a meeting held, say monthly, to talk about team and how each department was critical to the company's success. Only the sales team held meetings with leadership, except for meetings about what mistakes were made and or how a departments performance could be improved. Since the largest pool of revenue was for sales compensation, the support departments had employees that were hired for the least amount and expected to product the best. On top of that, new hires found out quickly, that team was not a part of the language in the company...it was Sales and All Others.

In later years, the company did eventually reconfigure the sales compensation to hire and train better support staff and eventually had more focus on team. The result; the company is a success today.

Example 2.

A family owned company with a sales team of about 40 and a total staff of about 160. When I got there the company had not been profitable in 7 out of 10 years or there about. The leadership team was family and a collection of people considered to be "key people" on the team. The problem was the "key people" were not on the team and the family leadership didn't know how out of control the culture was.

From day one... various people felt they had to warn me about who to watch out for and who to avoid...and there was a pool going on about how long I would last, based upon others who had taken the job previously.

The "Key People" ... leaked information to certain individuals on the sales team to gain favour and likeability...and to show that they were "in the know" ...and the leaks proved detrimental to any changes management wanted to make to help the company become more profitable. The sales team used the leaks to protest ahead of any changes and threaten the family with "we will leave..." There was a sycophant atmosphere involving a former sales manager that was now back in sales as his own choice...and he used this sycophant group to sabotage the family's management...and funny, shoot himself and the whole sales team, in the foot eventually.

This guy would regale anyone who would listen with tales of how great he was and how he could run the company better... and about how bad the company and the family were running the business. Instead of helping the company win, it became all about him. He was making up for a severe lack of self-esteem by making others around him wrong, so he could be right.

He never went to the family with any of his ideas to help them win, because if his ideas turned out to be wrong... (any many were), he would lose his cache.

This behaviour, led to the same poor behaviour by others on the sales team. It was not unusual to hear sales people shouting at support staff in the office and in front of others. The whole company descended into berating each other and complaining and management was indifferent to addressing any of the systemic culture issues. Even though bad behaviour was "the elephant in the room" … indifference became acceptance.

Everyone knew it was there and yet did nothing about it, except to complain among themselves and to others who could do nothing about it. It was water cooler talk. No one went to management about the key people leaking information and their sabotage… and no one stood up to any of the bullying. It seems incredulous even as I write it and I experienced it first- hand. When it involved me, I stood up and once one of the family members suggested that I not stand up to the former sales manager as they were afraid he would leave. My suggestion was this… "if someone wants a divorce, do you stay living with them…give him his divorce."

They were too afraid.

Eventually the company experienced extreme financial challenges as the sales force was over compensated, even at the expense of a reasonable company profit. Instead of implementing common sense cures, I was told "we cannot change any of the policy effecting the sales team because we promised them." They should have told the truth and said…" we are afraid of them."

The company was sold at a fire sale price. A sixty-year-old family business was lost to an out of control culture that said "don't mess with the sales team."

What would you prefer? A reasonable profit and a team environment with clear boundaries that say certain behaviours are not acceptable nor tolerated or a fire sale to a competitor?

Indifference equals acceptance in any situation and especially when out of bounds behaviour is tolerated. It says silently … we are ok with this. What I have seen in my 40+ years is that when these Narcissistic types are fired… the culture and the company not only survive them leaving…the company thrives and grows healthy amazingly fast.

Having a culture that is managed for individual respect with equal contribution from sales and sales support departments is critical to lightning success.

Leadership has a responsibility to check in on the culture by being proactive with training and also the message about "why" the company is in business. The team shares a common goal with differing responsibilities. What is the shared goal? Express it often, especially in management meetings. Express that in companywide meetings and step in immediately when behaviours by anyone, especially top performers, are out of bounds. Top performers need to lead by example with the best behaviours.

Sales meetings need to have support people attend as well, with open discussion about the shared goals and how they can all help each other reach the goals. How to help each other win. Perhaps having the sales team perform support roles from time to time, so that they really understand what support staff experiences in their jobs. This would help the sale team understand the challenges that the support team faces from customer and the challenges between departments.

Managing the culture is key to the lightning success of any company and especially for todays' leaders.

Culture was not even talk about when I entered the work world. It was "so the work and shut up." Support employees were just that.. employees and not people. Todays' leaders have a responsibility to provide for "self-growth" for the people they employ. Millennials expect training and support. Remember they are the generation where everyone went to their games and recitals and everyone got a medal, ribbon or a trophy. As our employees grow deeper roots and become better people, they make a larger contribution to the company and customers take notice. They like doing business with "adult companies and the adult people" who run them.

A part of any culture is the vision and language that is spoken. I am talking about a positive vision and language as compared to the negative. Small minded thinking has no part in the culture of a lightning growth company. As John Maxwell says "leaders need to think today of limitless possibilities." Limitless thinking can be taught and continually coached. Whether it's signage... to remind people of limitless possibilities or a training and coaching program, a monthly newsletter or all of the previous combined ... it's important to remind our people of the power they have if they can imagine anything is possible. Encourage limitless thinking in every meeting and address every challenge with "let's focus on the solutions to our challenges... what we focus on increases."

When, as a leader you hear limited possibility language, that is time to coach the staff with "hey, what happens if we look at this with limitless possibility thinking?" Challenge all the people to test it in their own lives. I have seen completely negative teams learn to challenge and push back against the negative, limited thinking and amaze themselves with what they accomplish once they switch to the positive and limitless. Imagine what effect a group of enthused, positive, limitless thinkers would have on your company and the growth? Besides managing the day to day operations and sales... it is an excellent investment in time and energy and it does take both... to manage your culture for lightning growth. Something that 20 years ago, was not talked about much.

Beginning with the end in mind, ask yourself, "what is the culture that you want to encourage and nurture?" Once you decide, consciously work towards that end...

every day. Do you have a positive culture that encourages personal growth, accountability, responsibility and respect toward all? Do you talk about a culture that supports everyone winning? How to help others be right as opposed to pointing out when one is wrong? Do you encourage everyone to go the extra mile in helping the company reach its' shared goals? Do you remind everyone that even the smallest things done well, with good intention make a difference? Even if its' cleaning up after yourself in the employee kitchen or in the restroom? That we build a great culture when we think about "who is next in the restroom and or the kitchen?

Everywhere we go, we all put out an energy that says "this is who I am." Do you think your actions go un-noticed? Think again. It's a cause and effect Universe. What you give anywhere you get… it will come back…it is coming back to you now.

We are always harvesting something we planted. What is the effect you desire and what is the cause that will bring that desired result?

Everything we think do and say is planting a seed for a future… isn't that enough of an argument to get you to look at your company's culture if you do not already do so?

Lightning Growth will include Culture Success Strategies and the work that goes into managing it…

Some stories of success;
My best and most memorable sales started at "no"

1. **Harvard University**

How this happened was my ability to detach from outcomes and be fully present with future clients. It was a natural skill and at the time it was not taught…I thought for sure if anyone found out I did this…I would have been fired…and look what happened in two instances…

> My best and most memorable sales started at no. I remember as I write this my first call with a sales rep that worked for me at Harvard University. The buyer, Linda, started our appointment with "We could never buy from you" …. I said, "Oh, I'm a little confused then, why did we get the appointment" ….
>
> I was very confused at that moment, wouldn't you be? I like to pay attention to what I am feeling and what I notice about the buyer's body language or facial expressions. I then find a way to say what I am feeling or noticing.

Linda replied to my question. "Oh, we heard a lot about your company and since you're new to Massachusetts, I figured we would find out about you."

I replied, "Oh, what did you hear"? She told me. I then asked "Linda, since we are not going to get the business, would you mind telling me all about what you are looking for and why we cannot get the business."

Linda replied "We currently have 16 suppliers and with some we have done business for over 30 years…so you see we could never give the business to you, we have never even done any business and we are going to select one supplier from the sixteen and consolidate all of our purchases.

I said, "That makes sense…it's probably what I would do" … "Would you mind telling me about your process of selection and what you are looking for the finalist to do for you?

She replied, "sure, no problem…"

Linda went on to tell me all about her process, what she was looking for her selected supplier to give her, etc….. over 45 minutes talking with someone who told me that we did not have a chance.

I ended our call with "you know Linda, it sounds to me like you're looking for a supplier partner" and she replied, "oh, partnership, what do you mean, would you explain that." I replied, "well, aren't all of your suppliers going to be coming in to your review and selection process" Linda replied "yes" …. I said, "why don't you wait and see if your current suppliers have the same idea and if not, call me I'll be glad to share it with you." She agreed that was fair.

Two weeks later, I got a phone call from Linda at Harvard, asking me to come in and explain my vision of a supplier partner. I said "sure Linda, would you do me a favour?" She replied "no problem, of course." I said "would you mind putting me on that list of suppliers that you are considering?"

She said "yes." Needless to say, I was on cloud nine that day.

Six months later, after a complete review of all the suppliers, and a bunch of work by a great team of people, WE GOT THE BUSINESS. THE COMPANY THAT LINDA SAID, "NO, WE COULD NEVER BUY FROM YOU" ….

We were awarded the contract for over $1 million dollars in annual sales….!!!!

2. Spaulding and Slye.

Six months later…I met Peter of Spaulding and Slye Real Estate management at a BOMA cocktail party and he saw my name badge and said "oh, you're with XXXX Paper company, we could never buy from you"'… and I said to Peter, "how do you know that I would sell you" ….

He was a little stunned and said "why wouldn't you sell us"? I asked him, "Do you sell everyone in your market" …he replied "no." I said, "why not?" Peter replied "well, not everyone is a fit…" and I asked "and that is because" …Peter replied "well, we cannot make money on every situation so we have to find out if we are a fit" …

I said to Peter, "Well it the same for us" …he understood. We spoke the rest of the evening and exchanged cards. I asked him before we parted, "how come you said that you could never buy from us…he said "oh, we have six or seven paper companies now and I am going to consolidate them to one and we have never even purchased from you" ….

Well, there is a lot more to the story and guess what happened a few weeks later? That's right, I got the business…over $750,000 annually…

What's more…when I got to Boston one year earlier I said to those around me "I am going to get Harvard and Spaulding & Slye" …
Funny how things work out…

Great things start at "no." It takes the pressure off of everyone. You can say what's important and the truth.

I say go for no in your conversations with Prospects. You cannot lose what you do not have anyway.

Go get 20 nos' today and 100 for the month and see what happens.

I wish you good selling.

Gratefully yours,
Steve

In Conclusion

Contrary to popular belief, selling does not have to be difficult. In fact, we are all programmed by nature to succeed with the least effort. If you are having trouble maintaining or growing your sales and commissions, give the steps above a try. If you are still finding sales difficult, honestly and brutally review what you have been planting in the way of activity or integrity, you are reaping that harvest. Use this book to prepare a new harvest and start planting new seeds now, right now.

I wish you an abundant harvest. Start planting.

With more than 40 years of sales and sales management experience, Stephen P. Lentini is CEO of Lentini Sales Leadership and Lord & Lentini Training Business and the Director of The Prosperity Institute, a business consulting and training company in Brooklyn, NY. He writes, teaches and trains on a variety of sales and management topics for audiences nationwide and Motivational Press has just published his first in a series of sales books titled "Sales Success for Rookies, How to Succeed at Sales Right from the Start" a book and CD program. The next book in the series is self-published and available on the web site at www.stevelentini.com "Sales Success for Veteran Sales People, **Gaining and Keeping An Edge to Close More Sales, More Often**

He is currently writing, teaching and developing other books, including "Wake up, Jump into your Life, "Sales Success for the Spiritual Sales Person, How to Sell Without Losing Your Soul".

Steve is a contributing author to "Imagine 30 Days to a New You, published in January 2016 and "Lightning Growth, Success Strategies for Today's Leaders, published January 2017 and both are published by Motivational Press with Justin Sachs and available on Amazon.

Selling and managing sales people for over forty years, Steve is author of the Sales Success Series of sales books, including Sales Success for the Rookie, How to Succeed at Sales Right from the Start and Sales Success for the Seasoned Sales Veteran, How to Stay at Peak Performance...and now this updated version "How to Gain and Keep an Edge to Close More Sales, More Often," as well as Wake up, Jump into Your Life and "Sales Success for the Spiritual Sales Person, How to Sell without Losing Your Soul."
Steve has owned a Wholesale Distribution business, Retails stores and a Consulting Practice. He held the license for the Sandler Sales Institute in Massachusetts from 1998 until 2003. His philosophy espouses the "no role play" method of sales training. Steve says "role play is un-necessary if you are totally present with your clients and there to genuinely help them, not sell them anything until you are sure that the both of you are a fit." "Sell the truth and if the truth won't sell, don't sell it is what I teach." Like Jim Rohn said, "the harder I worked on myself the better my business did."

I help my clients learn about the parts of themselves that they did not know, that they did not know."

Take your "self" on and succeed

www.ingramcontent.com/pod-product-compliance
Lightning Source LLC
Chambersburg PA
CBHW060436220526
45465CB00008B/3161